Folly

Polly

Memories of an East End Girl

JEFF SMITH

The
History
Press

First published 2012

The History Press
The Mill, Brimscombe Port
Stroud, Gloucestershire, GL5 2QG
www.thehistorypress.co.uk

© Jeff Smith, 2012

The right of Jeff Smith to be identified as the Author
of this work has been asserted in accordance with the
Copyrights, Designs and Patents Act 1988.

British Library Cataloguing in Publication Data.
A catalogue record for this book is available from the British Library.

ISBN 978 0 7524 6572 2

Typesetting and origination by The History Press
Printed in Great Britain

Contents

Introduction

Mary Rebecca Chambers (my mum, nicknamed Polly), was born on 10 August 1911 in Stratford, east London and was the fourth, but only the second surviving, child of Walter Robert and Mary Dorothy Chambers. They went on to have five more children and they all grew up as a close-knit family in the special community atmosphere which was London's East End. She lived in that area, mainly Stratford itself, for over fifty years and saw two world wars and the Great Depression from that unique perspective. Polly's was a life shaped and moulded by those times in an area that was so often at the sharpest of the sharp end of events, be that the grinding poverty of the Depression or the danger and disruption of aerial bombardment.

These events were deeply etched into her memory and she could be reminded of them at any time. For example, one day we saw one of the modern blimps that are now used for advertising and aerial photography. She glanced at it and casually remarked that 'the first time I saw one of those it was dropping bombs on me!' Similarly, some fifty or so years after the relevant events, we were sitting in the garden when the RAF Battle of Britain Memorial Flight (a Lancaster bomber accompanied by Spitfire and Hurricane fighters) just happened to pass by at low level behind her. Just the sound made her dissolve into tears, even though she could not see from whence it was coming – the sound itself was just too evocative.

Like so many of her generation, she was denied the chance of any more than the very minimum of a basic education and left school at the earliest possible legal age to earn a living and contribute to the family purse. Though she rarely spoke about it, she was keenly aware of this lost opportunity and its potential benefits. Perhaps as a result of this she was always the keenest proponent of education, especially for girls – 'educate a boy and he gets a better job, educate a girl and you educate a whole family' was one of her favourite sayings. Nevertheless, she was an acute observer of events around her, even if she sometimes had a very idiosyncratic view – she 'made her own arrangements about things' as she herself would say. Likewise, her stories are not always consistent, for example, her memory of her mother's cooking skills seemed to depend more on the needs of the particular story than any cool judgement.

As it happened, Polly was also one of nature's story tellers. She remembered events, situations and feelings, wove them into a pattern that made sense to her, and delighted to pass the tale on to others whenever she got the chance. Not surprisingly, for many listeners the stories were 'just ancient history' and their repetition tedious, but they fascinated me and I am pleased that I realised their value in time to write them down before her death in August 2000. This book is essentially a compilation of her stories, arranged in some sort of chronological order so that they tell the story of her life over those remarkable years. They are told the way she told them, using essentially the words she used, with no attempt to make them historically or factually consistent. Very occasionally I have added my own comment or explanation. Also, in some cases where the subject matter was closely related or sensibly 'followed on' I have run a couple of her stories together into a single account. Many of the stories overlapped with each other but no attempt has been made to disentangle them – they are just presented as they were. Ultimately, this was the way she remembered her very ordinary life that was, in fact, quite remarkable in momentous times.

Jeff Smith, 2012

1

Origins and Early Days

(1900–12)

My grandparents came from Hoxton in the East End of London. Grandad had been a farrier, then a carman, and ended up as a piano-remover, which tells you something about how different life was then. For some reason he lost his job and things got tough for a while, but Grandma was a real worker and started to take in washing. Very soon she could afford to have a shed built in the backyard to house some washtubs and she employed some women to come in two days a week to do the washing. There was no heating, but they worked out there in all weathers, even when there was snow on the ground. Mum used to get quite upset and say that Grandma was wicked, but Grandma didn't care. The women she employed didn't care either. For the little bit of extra money they would have come in seven days a week in any weather if they could. Grandma did all the finishing work herself, and she had all the different special irons for doing cuffs, lace, collars, the lot. She worked hard all week, but once finished on a Friday night she would take herself over to the pub and pretty well stay there until Sunday night. Mum said that she even cooked the Sunday lunch from there, telling the kids when to put the joint in the oven, when to turn it over, and in between they would take a bowl of potatoes over to be peeled, then the peas for shelling, and so on.

When Mum and Dad got married they decided to move away from their parents and go off into the country. So they moved to a country cottage down

Mary Dorothy Barker – Mum – pictured in about 1905.

Mortham Street in Stratford. You can't imagine it now because Stratford is as much part of the East End as Hoxton. To be honest, I couldn't believe it myself when I grew up in the 1920s and '30s because it was already a bit of dirty, industrial, London sprawl and there was no country until past Ilford. Later though, after the Second World War, we lived just around the corner from there, so I went for a walk down to the end of Mortham Street. Sure enough, there was a row of little cottages. By then they were surrounded by London terraces, just like all the rest, but you could see that once they had been in the country – they just had that look about them. So Mum wasn't exaggerating after all.

Stratford Broadway around the time of Polly's birth.

When they got married Dad used to work in the Borough Market but by the time they moved to Mortham Street he was working in Stratford Market so it was quite convenient really, but they decided that it was too quiet out in the country after the hustle and bustle of London. About that time the Carpenters Company decided to develop the land they owned in Stratford and they launched on an ambitious project to build a whole new residential area. I suppose it would be called a New Town these days. That was the start of the Carpenters Road estate and it was the most modern thing you could imagine then – every house had its own water supply and a toilet that you could flush with a chain. They also built a school for the children and public baths – it was out of this world. It was also nearer London, so Mum and Dad moved there and took a house next door to Mum's aunt.

The trouble with Mum's aunt was that she was always borrowing things. Every day she was in for a cup of this or a bowl of that and in the end Mum got fed up with it. So one day she decided to move away. It all seems ever so lax and hit-or-miss these days, but she did not make any plans or arrangements. There was a house empty more or less across the road, so after Dad had gone to work she just set to and moved everything across the road. That afternoon she had to stand on the doorstep to catch Dad when he came home. Mind you, that house had its disadvantages too. There was a dairy just down the road (can you imagine a dairy in Carpenters Road?) and the fields were a bit further up the other way. So every morning and every evening the cows were brought past Mum's windows, to and from the dairy, to be milked. Then the horses that pulled the milk carts were brought along the same route. She did not put up with that for long and moved back across the road but a bit further up and this was the house where they started their family.

My sister Doll was the first to be born, then came another daughter. When she was about three she took ill and eventually Mum had to call the doctor – a serious decision because doctors had to be paid so you only called them in an emergency. The doctor sent the baby straight off to hospital. On Christmas Day, as Mum was serving up the Christmas dinner, two policemen arrived on the doorstep to tell Mum she should go up to the hospital – sadly her daughter had died that Christmas afternoon. Mum was pregnant at the time and the baby (I think it was a boy) was born prematurely a couple of months later. The poor little blighter was blind and did not have much of a chance – they just didn't have all the medical services in those days. He lived for a couple of days though, but that meant that when he died they had to have a proper funeral for him as well. So Mum had funerals for two of her children within a couple of months of each other. I was the next one born, but that is the reason there is such a big gap between me and my eldest sister – there should have been two others in between.

I can just about remember Grandma. She did very well with her laundry business and, if the truth be told, earned more than Grandad. She was quite comfortably off at the end. I can remember her coming to visit us at least once a week, always dressed in the same way. On her head she always wore a black bonnet. During the week it was a plain one but on Sundays she had a Sunday best, trimmed with ribbons. Then she had a black cape that was trimmed with beads and braid, and a long black skirt which went down almost to the ground. What fascinated me as a kid, though, were her long, black, button-up boots. I used to think they were wonderful, and it was always my ambition to have a pair myself. By the time I was old enough, though, they were completely out of fashion and I never did get a pair.

2

The First World War

(1914–18)

I was barely three when the First World War started but that is the cause of my earliest memory. We lived in a half-house in Lett Road at the time, and were very lucky to have that much to live in. I suppose Dad had a good job, as jobs went at that time. He was a market porter in Stratford, which meant that at least we always had food on the table. He used to enjoy his beer and usually came home the worse for wear, I suppose it was part of the way of life down the market, but he always made sure Mum had enough money to feed us. We had the upstairs half of the house and the kitchen opened off the landing at the top of the stairs looking straight down to the front door.

When I was little Mum used to stand me in a bowl on the kitchen table for my wash before bedtime. I could stand there and watch down the stairs to the front door. This particular evening I was watching when Dad came in. He looked a bit different; I suppose he was fully sober for a change. He came up the stairs, into the kitchen and stood, looking a bit uncomfortable. Mum carried on washing me, until at last he broke the silence.

'I've done it Doll,' he said.

That was all he had to say. I suppose he and Mum had talked about the war and what he was going to do, and no doubt Mum had made clear what she thought about it. There was silence. Mum lost all interest in me and just looked, though goodness knows where she was looking. Then suddenly she took the flannel she had been using on me and flung it down on the ground between Dad's feet.

'You stupid bastard,' she said, and that was that.

I didn't know what was going on, I was still a baby really, but even I could tell this was something important. It did not take Mum long to regain her composure and then the fireworks started.

'What did you do that for? You can't just walk out like that . . . What am I supposed to do with the children [there were three of us then]? You silly bugger, you'll get killed . . .' And so it went on. It did not take long to develop into a full-scale fight between the two of them. Not that my mother needed much excuse for a row anyway. If she wanted to, she could have started an argument with the stones in the street. I cannot recall how it ended and how I eventually went to bed. Of course, I had no idea what it was all about. How should I know what 'volunteered' meant, what was 'war' that kept being shouted, in fact how should I know what adults were talking about at any time. However, I think that was the moment I became aware that the world and other people were something different and separate from me. Up until then I had just accepted them as part of what happened to me, but now I realised that they had their own existence – from that moment I started to grow up.

Those stairs figured again a couple of years later. Dad was away in the army by now and we barely ever saw him. Buying food was difficult and you had to know where to go, which shop had what available, and then be prepared to queue for it. Mum had gone shopping and, along with my baby brother, I was left at home in the care of my big sister. Our baby brother was the first boy in the family and so all his life was known as 'Son'. Anyway, our street door was the typical half-glazed sort, all the houses in the street had them. It had leaded lights, and in our door most of them were red with a narrow strip of plain glass like a border. I used to like sitting on the stairs looking through the translucent red at the street beyond. Really it was too dark to make anything out clearly but you could see the shapes of people going by and hear the noises. On this particular day I was sitting on the stairs looking at the window in the door and waiting for Mum to come home to cook some tea. Suddenly the door lit up. The whole world lit up. I looked around and the whole house was red light. I wondered what was happening. It was amazing. I was completely surrounded by red light; everything was red light. And then it faded until, after a couple of seconds, there was a distant rumble. That was the Silvertown Explosion, when a huge store of explosives being stockpiled for the war went up by accident [Editor's note: January 1917].

As I said, getting food became very difficult and queueing became a way of life. Once, I think it was when Dad was coming home on leave, Mum decided that she wanted a good piece of meat for the occasion. She was working by then and had to go out early in the morning. So on this particular day I was got up at about six in the morning and went down to wait in the butcher's queue. That takes some thinking about because I could have only been about five, or maybe six, at the time. I stayed in the queue until my sister Doll came along at about half past seven. She had got our brother up, dressed him, and after having some breakfast taken him downstairs to the lady who looked after him during the day. She also made some toast and tea for me and it was left ready on the table when she came to take her turn in the queue. Then I went home to have breakfast. Doll queued until Mum came back from work on her 'breakfast break' to buy the joint when the shop finally opened. Meanwhile, Doll came back to collect me and off we went to school – all to get a decent joint of meat.

Luckily, though getting food was difficult, Mum had the knack of making a decent meal out of anything or nothing. I can still remember the recipe for a meal for four from two (or even, one) cod heads. You boil and mash a good pile of potatoes. Meanwhile boil the heads in milk and when cooked pick off every bit of meat and 'soft stuff' you can find. Use the milk to make a white sauce with lots of parsley (if you can find any). Then mix in all the fish meat and pour it over the mashed potato. We used to think that was a great treat, though I am not sure that you could put it in front of anybody today!

Nothing was easy during the war and there was nothing like the medical services we have now. I remember when Son and I were ill at one time – I think it was in one of those 'flu epidemics that caused so many deaths. We were so ill that we could not go to school, though Doll seemed to go through untouched. Anyway, us two could not go to school but Mum could not afford to miss a day's work – if you did not work you did not get paid, it was as simple as that. So she tucked us up in bed as warmly as she could each day and off she went. We were not getting any better though, and I think she was beginning to get worried so she started thinking about getting the doctor round. Trouble was, doctors cost one-and-six a visit and Mum just did not have the money. She was talking about this at work and one of the women told her that, because her husband was away in the army, if she went to the RO (Relief Office) she would get a doctor's visit for free. So off she went, queued up for ages, and finally got in to see the clerk. She explained her problem, at which point the clerk asked why she had come to the RO.

Dolly and Polly (seated) in about 1915 on a postcard to be sent to Dad at the front.

'Well, I haven't got any money' she replied.

'But you have got a wedding ring haven't you,' he said, pointing at her finger, 'Pawn that first before you say you haven't got any money!'

Can you imagine it? Mum was really scandalised and walked out. Instead she came home and told us we could have any toy in the toy-shop if we got better. I think that really she just begrudged giving any money to doctors. We did both recover and Mum went and got some money from the Provident to buy our promised toys. Son got a trolley full of building blocks and I got a dolly. I had that dolly for years and loved it more than words can tell. Mind you, I think Mum was paying off the club for the rest of the year, if not the rest of the war!

While Dad was away in the war we only saw him once in the next four years. I don't know much about what he did and what happened to him during the war, though I know that at one time he volunteered to be the cook for his regiment or unit or whatever it was. Perhaps he felt it was safer to be away from the shooting. It might have been safer for him but I am not sure about the rest of the soldiers. He only had the job a short while – apparently one day some of the men killed some rabbits and said that they would really like a rabbit stew. He had no idea what to do so threw the rabbits into the pot, skinned but still with their furry feet on and complete with their innards! He was court-martialled for that and returned to more regular duties. He did see some action though. I remember him talking about 'going over the top' and for some reason I think it was that awful Somme battle. Anyway, he said he left his trench and marched straight ahead towards the enemy lines with bullets flying all around him. It was pretty bad so he stopped to look around him and suddenly realised that he was the only one left standing! It did not take him a second to realise that this was too dangerous so he quickly laid himself down in the nearest shell-hole and stayed there until it was dark. Then he made his way back to his own lines. I suppose that if he had told his story it would have been called cowardice or something, but there were so few survivors from his regiment that nobody had the nerve to ask him how he managed it. I don't know if that was the occasion, but for years the pride of place on our mantelpiece at home was taken by his cap-badge, with its top half carried away by a bullet. It went straight through the hat he was wearing without even ruffling his hair!

It must have shaken him a bit though and I think that may have been the reason he got a thirteen-day leave. On the first morning of his leave, Mum got us – that is me, Doll and our Son – up early and dressed us in our Sunday best. After breakfast we went straight down to Stratford Market station (it is not there any longer) and stood on the platform to wait for Dad. We waited all morning and trains came and trains went. Lots of soldiers got off and were welcomed with hugs and kisses and tears, but no Dad. Mum had given us some sandwiches and we had our lunch sitting on the platform. Then we waited all afternoon but it was the same story as the morning. Eventually it began to get a bit dark and we had to go home for dinner. We stayed up for a long time but there was still no Dad and so Mum sent us to bed. I don't know how long we slept but it was well into the night when I heard Dad come in. I heard his voice talking to Mum for a couple of moments and then he came straight into us. I was awake anyway but he just grabbed me, Doll and our Son and hugged us. He was crying, something I had never seen before or since. I suppose he thought he would never see us again. Doll and I were crying too, but our Son was too young to know what was going on. He just kept moaning that Dad's whiskers were covered with snow and made him cold!

That was the longest, or was it the only, stretch we saw of him during the war. I remember that one night he and Mum went up the music hall in Stratford to see a show, but it got interrupted by a Zeppelin raid. Mum came rushing back

Walter Robert Chambers – Dad – in uniform.

to see to us kids but Dad stayed to see the end of the show and later ambled home as if he did not have a care in the world. I suppose that, compared to the trenches, the odd small bomb thrown from an airship and aimed at the whole of London, was not much of a threat. Anyway, Mum left a note for Dad and rushed us off down to the shelter. When these Zeppelin raids started the authorities decided that they needed some sort of shelters and so they started designating large, sturdy, buildings – which in Lett Road meant the factories a bit further down. Would you believe it, our appointed shelter was a paint and varnish factory, complete with all its stocks of paint and solvents. The shelter was on the ground floor below them all – you say it now and it sounds crazy. If a bomb had hit it we would have all been fried or burned alive, but at the time we only saw it as a large, strong building. I suppose we were very naïve then, we learnt better in the next war.

When the raid ended we set off to go back home and found Dad sat on one of our kitchen chairs under the railway arch, with the bread board on his knees and on it half a loaf and the remains of the joint. He was steadily working his way through it all. Mum went off at him about not being stupid and that he should have gone down to the shelter, but he replied that people and paint factories were not very important to the war effort, but railways were. So, if anything went wrong, they would be out straight away to deal with damage to a railway bridge but you could not say the same for a paint factory. Looking back, I realise that Dad had seen it at the sharp end and knew a lot more about war than us. He was almost certainly right. But also, when I look back, it frightens me to think what could have happened in that shelter if it had been hit by any sort of bomb at all!

One of the factories down the road was used for housing prisoners of war. They used to be marched down our road, but beforehand we were all instructed to stay indoors, close all doors, windows and curtains and stay out of sight until they had passed. This was all too much for my curiosity and I used to go to the front bedroom and peek round the very edge of the curtain, trying not to disturb it or be seen. I was always surprised because 'the prisoners' looked just like ordinary men. I think I really expected them to have hooves, or tails, or something, not just to be ordinary, tired-looking men. In one of the Zeppelin raids the factory where they were held was hit. The bomb landed on the gatehouse and killed one of the guards; he was the only casualty. You should have heard everybody going on about it though – they really thought that the Zeppelin had aimed at the gatehouse and that somehow it was typical of the nasty Germans.

Dad went all through the war and came back without a scratch. In fact, the regular food and physical training built him up a lot. He had gone into the army as a short, slim man who took quite a pride in his appearance. He was quite a sharp dresser in his own way. He came back looking more like a barrel, and his mates back at the market gave him the nickname 'Mudguts'. My brother Bob, the first of the post-war family, was born nine months to the day after Dad was demobbed.

3

School

(1915–25)

Dad volunteered for the army almost as soon as the war began and we didn't see much of him for the next four years. He used to send his army pay home or maybe they arranged to pay it direct to Mum, I don't know which, but it wasn't good money in any sense. It was nothing like the market pay and had none of the perks that went with it either, so Mum was soon feeling the pinch. That was when she decided to get a job. Of course, getting a job was easy because there was so much war work with all the men gone. The big problem was what to do with us children but that was soon solved. Doll was already at school and though I was only four the school agreed that I could go as well. Mind you, I went to the infants while Doll was in the 'real school'. Then the baby, Son (and he kept that nickname all his life!), was looked after by the woman who lived downstairs in the other half of the house we shared.

I still remember my first day. I put on my best clothes and Mum took me up to the school to look around. First of all we met Miss Gray, who was the governess – that is, the headmistress – and she showed us around. I remember the hall because there, tied up in the corner, was the most perfect swing you can ever imagine. Us kids, living and playing in the streets, never really saw a swing except now and again when we went to the park. But here was a proper swing, right in the school. What was more, Miss Gray told us that on Friday afternoon, if the children had been good, they came into the hall and had a swing. Well, I think I must have been the best-behaved child that they ever had in that school, but I never got a turn on that swing. That was all I lived for and my every action was aimed towards having a turn on it, but it never happened. I think I have held that against the school ever since, and it is still the first thing that comes into my mind about my schooldays.

Apart from that, school was not at all bad. In fact, I think I rather enjoyed going to school and nothing sticks out as being a bad time. I suppose it was wartime and there is always a bit of excitement, but as kids you enjoy the excitement without thinking about the dangers and threats. Talking of which, we did have some 'raids' and they caused ever such a stir.

As I said, I was in the infants, and we used to finish every day at 4 p.m. I used to go and wait in the playground until 4.15 p.m. which was when Doll finished. I would wait there come rain or shine, hail or snow, and honestly I didn't think anything of it. When Doll came out we would walk home together and then have a load of jobs to do; peeling the potatoes and things like that in preparation for when Mum got in and cooked the tea.

Anyway, early one afternoon there was a raid, goodness knows whether it was a Zeppelin or aeroplanes, though I do remember seeing Zeppelins at some point during the war. We children all had to climb under our desks, which we thought was ever such an adventure. The Germans dropped a torpedo – I don't know whether it was a torpedo, a bomb, a landmine or what, but we called them all 'torpedoes' – on a factory down the other end of the road. As I said, we thought it was ever so exciting but the teachers were absolute nervous wrecks. It was all too much for them, so it was decided to shut the school and send us home. Trouble was, lots of mothers went out to work so they didn't know whether the kids could get indoors, whether anybody was there to look after them and all that. It was decided that nobody could go home until somebody came to collect them. This was terrible, because Mum worked at the other end of Stratford and so was not likely to hear that the school had closed. Fortunately the lady downstairs came up to collect her daughter and I saw her across the hall. After a few words with the governess she was allowed to take us home, so I went to find Doll and off we went.

The woman downstairs was a bit funny. To tell the truth, I think she was a bit simple and the bloke she married was a real rough piece of work. But he suited her and they seemed to get on alright, which is about all that matters. I think she was too simple to realise anything different was possible. That simplicity was what carried her through life and nothing seemed to get to her, nothing upset her, nothing got on the wrong side of her. For all that, she was a kindly woman and would do anything she could to help without thinking that she was doing anything at all. You couldn't take any sort of exception to her. One of her oddities, though, was that every day she used to wear a coarse apron and a man's cloth cap.

Anyway, on this day she came up to the school for her kid and so she took us home as well. We were ever so pleased to see her. It was quite a while later that Mum turned up. She wasn't very much earlier than if she had finished work as usual, but it seemed to take that long for the word to get round Stratford about the school closing. She came rushing home to see if we were OK, and of course we were having a great time playing with the woman's daughter. We told her the story and suddenly she absolutely hit the roof. No word of thanks about the woman collecting and looking after us, no appreciation or anything. Mum was just so disgusted that this woman would collect her children wearing a coarse apron and cloth cap! She was disgusted beyond words and was leading off something rotten. She could have saved her breath though, because the woman downstairs just stood there smiling, nodding her head, and saying, 'yes, Mrs Chambers, oooh yes, Mrs Chambers, oooh, I do agree,' and so on. I don't suppose she had the faintest idea what Mum was going on about and how ungrateful she was being, but that is why I say her simplicity carried her through life.

That raid was on a Wednesday, and there was another on the following Sunday. We called them 'Torby-Wednesday' and 'Torby-Sunday' – 'Torby' was our East End abbreviation of torpedo! That was about all I remember of the war and school. If the truth be told, I think I quite enjoyed it all.

Soon after the war we saw our first aeroplane. The whole school was rapidly ushered out into the playground to witness the amazing sight and we all stood there peering into the sky. Then the aeroplane wrote something using that smoke stuff. I can't remember what it wrote, but three of the girls fainted with the wonder of it all. They must have thought that words in the sky was a sign that the world was ending! The other big excitement, for me anyway, was bath day. None of the houses around there had a bath, so every week ten children were taken off to the public baths in Jupp Road. We were called out of class, formed up in the playground and were led off in a crocodile to the baths. When we got there we undressed and put our clothes in a locker before going on to the cubicles where our baths had already been filled by the attendant. There were no taps on the bath but instead, if you wanted more water, you would call out 'number-whatever, more hot water' and it would arrive out of a pipe through the wall. I used to love that.

What I really remember, though, was the Depression that followed the war – that truly was awful. When he came out of the army, Dad went straight back into his job in the market. This was secure, paid good money and had very useful perks, so we had no problems. In fact compared with the people who lived around us we were pretty well-off. Lots of men, though, were unemployed and had no real prospect of work. They lived from hand to mouth in a state of destitution. Boys used to come to school wearing baggy trousers and a vest. The trousers were held up by rope, tied either as a belt or over the shoulders as braces. They had to have something on their feet, bare feet were not allowed, so most had boots but no socks. Sometimes they would tie the laces together and hang the boots round their necks, putting them on when they got to the school gate, just so that they didn't wear out so quickly.

Most children didn't have much in the way of food either. Just to give an example, there was the time that I was picked for the school netball team. I was ever so proud and even Mum seemed pleased. Usually she didn't worry too much about what was going on at school as long as I was not 'getting into trouble', so you can believe that this was a special occasion. But then I discovered the catch – the practices were held at lunchtime so I had to tell the teacher that I couldn't be in the team after all. You see, Mum was pregnant and getting near her time, so I had to go home for lunch and then go to the shops to buy the dinner for Mum to cook in the evening. I got a terrible reputation for being 'stuck up' and not caring about the team, because they just did not believe me – they couldn't believe that somebody had lunch, let alone dinner as well. Most of them lived on bread and a scrape for breakfast and maybe the same, or some boiled potatoes, for dinner. For them, lunchtime netball practice was at least something to do and help fill the time, because the poor sods had nothing to go home for and fill their tummies!

Dad working in the market had other benefits. When I was ill once he came in to see me and asked if there was anything I wanted, some grapes or something. Well, I didn't want anything to eat, but I really wanted some flowers. I knew that posh grown-ups got flowers as presents and I wanted the same. It was early in the year, springtime, and blow me down if he didn't turn up from work that evening with a box – yes, a whole box – of daffodils. From that day I have always loved yellow flowers, especially daffodils. I suppose he got them cheap, if he paid for them at all, but he was always generous over that sort of thing. Our Bob had a friend who was run over and killed by a car. It was all dreadfully sad. Somehow in those days the communities seemed much closer together, and an accident like that touched everybody. Anyway, for the funeral

Mum and Dad on holiday in the late 1930s.

Dad got a whole box of chrysanths from the market. I thought it would be a good idea to keep some of them for the house – after all, nobody would notice a couple of bunches missing from a whole box. Mum was horrified at me, and completely adamant, 'Those flowers was bought for Billy Hoskins and Billy Hoskins would have them – ALL!'

There was always great excitement when it snowed – not for us kids but among the unemployed men. They would all rush off straight down to the Council Offices and see if they could get taken on for snow clearing – it was about the only work that many of them could get. Those taken on would be given their streets and go out to spend the day shovelling snow. You have to remember that they were dreadfully poor, most of them couldn't afford any proper warm clothes. Can you imagine shovelling snow all day wearing a vest, jacket and scarf, thin trousers, no socks but only a pair of thin shoes (maybe with holes in) on your feet and no gloves on your hands?

Mum was always generous to these poor devils. She used to keep an eye on the street from the front bedroom window and would give them a hot drink when they got as far as our house. We had the top half of the house and the stairs led straight down to the front door. One day Mum went downstairs to talk to a snow clearer and after a couple of moments came back upstairs, made a mug of cocoa and sandwich and went back down. I stood in the kitchen doorway to watch what was going on but she shouted at me to shut the door and keep the warmth in. I was being nosey, though, so I went out onto the landing and shut the door behind me. That way I could stand in the shadow and still watch what was going on at the front door. I don't know whether Mum knew I was there or could still see me, but I thought that I was hiding. Anyway, she gave this man the cocoa and sandwich and he came in and sat on the foot of the stairs. He was shivering like nobody I had ever seen, or have ever seen since, I think. At first, he could barely get the sandwich into his mouth because he couldn't control his teeth. Anyway, Mum stayed talking to him until he finished the food and got up to leave. The poor bloke didn't seem to know enough ways of saying 'thank you', and I suddenly realised that he was actually bowing to MY MUM!

'Thanks lady,' he said one more time, 'you saved my life.' I think he meant it.

Jobs were impossible to find and men would do anything for the chance of work. There was a woodyard at the far end of the street, Glikstens I think it was. They had a couple of vacancies, nothing special – just a couple of men to work in the yard fetching and carrying. Normally these sort of jobs were snapped up as soon as they became available by somebody telling somebody as soon as anything was known. This time, though, they wanted to do it 'properly' and so they were stupid enough to advertise the jobs in the local paper, telling candidates to present themselves for interview on a certain date. Well, late in the afternoon of the day before that, a steady procession of men started going past our front door. One of them sat on our front wall for a rest and so

Mum gave him a cup of tea. We could barely understand what he said in reply because his accent was so thick. It turned out that he had walked, yes walked, from Newcastle-upon-Tyne to try for this job. From then on Mum stood at the front door, pretty well until bedtime, giving out cups of tea to anybody who asked. We kids ran up and downstairs with empty cups, washing up, fetching more milk and whatever. We were absolutely forbidden to go outside, though. By the time we got up next morning there were more people than I had ever seen in the street. Apparently Glikstens were horrified by the size of the crowd, and anyway they had no way of dealing with so many applicants, so they put a notice on the gate to say that they didn't have any vacancies after all. The result was disaster. Well, you can imagine, such a huge crowd of desperate men, some of them had walked the length of the country, along with all those who had been queueing since the day before and through the night. There was a riot, no other word for it. In the end the men broke into the yard and set light to it. I don't know whether it was an accident or deliberate, but the result was the same. Of course, the fire engines took ages to get through the crowds who were not feeling very cooperative anyway. By the time they got there the yard was ablaze from end to end and there was nothing to be done. It burned right through the night and well into the next day before they got it under control.

The police were called and had to quell the riot and control the crowd. Mum had sent me up to Stratford on some errand and when I got back there was a rope barrier across the end of Lett Road. I didn't think about it and ducked under the rope to go home. Suddenly this policeman called out and came chasing after me. I was dead scared, but when I explained I lived there he got another policeman to walk all the way home with me. A little while later there was a man sitting on our front wall, so Mum went to see what he was up to and send him on his way. Instead she took pity and asked if he would like a cup of cocoa. I will always remember his reply – 'I'd even like a glass of water, lady.'

He must have been in a bad way because Mum invited him in to sit on the bottom of our stairs while she got the cocoa. Then she noticed his feet. He had the remains of a pair of boots wrapped round them, and inside those were some tatters of an old pair of cotton socks stuck to his feet by the dried blood. So she sent me to boil a kettle, then bring a bowl of hot water, then bring a flannel, then bring scissors to cut off the remains of the socks, then bring a towel. Mum was soft-hearted but never did anything herself – she supervised while others did all the fetching and carrying! To crown it all, she even dug out an old pair of Dad's socks and an old pair of boots before she sent him on his way. Dad hit the roof when he got home.

Over the next day or so the men gradually drifted away and the street became quiet again. I will never forget the desperation of those men that brought them from the other end of the country to start a riot in our street.

4

A Woman on the Bus

(1916)

One day, a couple of years after the war [Editor's note: Second World War], I was upstairs on the bus and started talking to this woman who happened to be sitting next to me. Goodness knows who she was, I'd never seen her before or since, but she was about the same age as me and grew up in the same places as me, so we had a lot of experiences in common. We were talking about how things used to be, how tough our early lives had been, how grim life had been in the First World War, the Depression, and so on and on, when we passed the City of London Cemetery. The woman looked straight past me at the cemetery and went all misty-eyed. For a couple of moments she sat silently watching the cemetery going past. Suddenly she said, 'My baby brother is buried in there.' Well, it wasn't unusual for little babies to die back then; we didn't have the medical services to care for babies either during the birth or if they got little colds or other illnesses afterwards. As often as not you couldn't afford to get a doctor anyway, unless things were really bad, and then it was often too late. Even so, it didn't make any difference that baby deaths happened so often – they were never any easier to cope with.

Her brother's death had obviously affected this woman terribly and so I made some comforting noises about how awful it must have been, and how difficult it used to be for everybody, how babies used to die because we could not afford doctors, and so on, when she broke in, 'It wasn't like that!' And what a story she went on to tell! She admitted that most of her story had been put together afterwards, because at the time she was too young to realise quite what was going on. Her mother had never said anything about it and had refused to talk about it, so she had gradually made sense of the events she remembered as she grew up and her understanding increased.

Her mother had been pretty young, barely much of a teenager herself, and it seems that she had met this fellow who had a good job and in a matter of months they were married. They moved into a couple of rooms, which was good going when lots of just-marrieds had to live with one or other set of parents. Nine months later the first child was born – the woman that I was talking to. Within a very short time the First World War broke out and the woman's father joined up. So, within little more than a year, this woman's mother had met a man, married him, had his child and he was gone again. Looking back, it was clear that she had no idea at all how to cope with her life, though thankfully she still had her mother's support.

Anyway, over the next couple of years they had quite a struggle to get by. She thought her father visited once or twice, he must have got leave sometimes, but she wasn't completely sure. Then she gradually became aware that something was up. Her mother wasn't very well, was beginning to get fat and there were all sorts of whispered conversations. She could see that her mother was dreadfully upset and she stopped going out. Instead her grandmother used to get all the shopping and she came round for long conversations, sometimes arguments. Her face was always cross and she barely spoke to her granddaughter. Eventually, her mother sat her down to tell her a 'very important secret'. She was told it was terribly, terribly secret and that she must never tell anyone – not even her father! She was going to have a little brother or sister, but no one must ever know. She could not understand how nobody was ever to know, especially her father when he came home again, but she accepted what her mother had said. Her grandmother kept coming round and doing all the jobs that meant going out, but kept just as stony-faced as ever.

Eventually the day came; her mother kept getting pains and took to her bed. The daughter, even though she was only a couple of years old, could see that there was something wrong and wanted to get help, but her mother said not to worry, grandma would soon be there. Eventually grandma turned up, went in to see the mother, came out again and set about collecting 'things' together. She told the little girl to play, to be an especially good girl, and not to go into the bedroom. The grandma stayed much later than usual, in fact right into the night. At bedtime grandma put her to bed on two chairs in the living room. She didn't sleep very well and kept hearing shouts and yells from her mother, sobs, grandma's hardest voice, and eventually a baby's cries.

Her grandma was still there next morning when she woke up. Grandma made some breakfast and told the girl that every thing was alright and that her mother would just need a couple of days' rest.

'What about my little brother?' she asked (she said that she 'just knew' it would be a little boy), but grandma just said something about not being a time for silly questions and she should eat her breakfast. And that was that. For the next couple of days grandma was there for almost the whole time. The girl went in to see her mother a couple of times but she looked perfectly well enough to a three-year-old. Then her mother got up and grandma went home. The girl kept asking about her baby brother, but only ever got answers to completely different questions.

The day after her mother got up for the first time she woke her daughter very early and said they were going for a walk. They were going to take her baby brother out – and this was the first and only time the baby was mentioned – but it was all still 'a great secret'. Her mother said that she would have the special job of looking after her brother, but still she must not tell anybody about it. After a quick breakfast her mother dressed her up very warmly – it was winter – and put her in the pushchair. Her mother then tucked a very tight bundle in beside her, and somehow she realised this was her brother but couldn't understand why she could not see his face. Her mother then wrapped and tucked her and the bundle into the pushchair with two or three blankets. She had never been so tightly wrapped in and could barely move. With one more warning about 'the secret' they went out. It was very early, in fact it was still dark and there weren't many people about. They, or rather, her mother, walked for miles and after a while it began to get light. It was a cold, drizzly, dreary, morning but her mother didn't seem to notice and just pushed on as fast as she could walk. They were walking up a long, tree-lined, street when a lorry went past them and then stopped a few yards ahead. There were a lot of soldiers in the back and they started calling out to them.

'Come on!' they shouted, 'jump in, we will give you a lift, can't have a good looker like you wandering the streets this time of the morning,' and so on. Her mother looked terrified. She made an excuse about the pushchair but that was no problem and two soldiers jumped down and lifted pushchair, the girl and her unseen brother into the back of the lorry. There was nothing for it and the mother climbed on the back of the lorry and sat in the space the soldiers had made for her. She grasped the handle of the pushchair and looked at her daughter with a combination of utter terror and direct threat to keep silent. Looking back, she realised that her mother must have been thinking about these soldiers and worrying about whether they knew her husband. Suppose they talked to him and told him the story? Really, it was totally stupid. When you think how many soldiers were fighting the war it was unbelievable that these men would somehow come across her husband, but she was young and naïve and thought that all the soldiers knew each other! She got more and more agitated with each minute that passed and looked as though she was going to cry.

They didn't stay on the lorry for long. Her mother suddenly said this was where they were going and the soldiers helped them off again. They shot off in the opposite direction, round the first corner, and stopped. After a couple of minutes her mother looked back round the corner and, seeing nothing, they set off on their way again. Eventually they reached some gates, which she now realised belonged to the cemetery. They were closed, I suppose they weren't unlocked until 8 o'clock or something. They stood in a doorway up the road until the gates were unlocked and when the keeper had walked away they went in. Her mother pushed her somewhere far from the gates to where there were some trees. She parked her daughter under the trees looking down one of the roadways and said she should watch to see if anybody came. Then her mother disappeared into the trees, urgently digging down into her shopping bag. After some while she came back, pulled out the blankets, took the bundle and disappeared again. After a bit longer she came back again, obviously crying, tucked her daughter into the pushchair and they retraced their steps back home, this time rather more slowly.

Her baby brother was never mentioned again. She had kept the secret until today, talking to a total stranger on top of a bus. She could only wonder at the terror of her poor young mother trying to work out what to do with this unwanted unwelcome baby and the desperation of that journey to the cemetery. But she could never stop wondering about that baby's cry in the night.

5

Standard of Living

(1920–8)

Ido get fed up with all these scientists who find out that this or that food
is bad for you. Every type of food seems to take turns at being bad for
you – nowadays coffee is one of the big villains but when I was at school
it was tea, and I once won a prize for an essay about the dangers and evils
of tea drinking. The teacher gave us a lesson about it, full of warnings about
the tannin and how it attacked the lining of your stomach, and goodness
knows what else, and then everybody in the class had to write an essay for the
competition. It was for all the schools in London. As far as I can remember it
wasn't the first prize that I won, but it was something.

Mind you, tea in those days was always terribly stewed and I dread to think
what was in it by the time you drank it. You see, tea was expensive so it never
got wasted. Instead, when tea was made the teapot was put onto the hot plate
and just kept going with more tea and water all day so that when anybody
came in they were immediately offered a cup of tea. Old Mrs M used to go
even further and every night she would pour the remains of that day's tea into
a jug, which she kept on the dresser. Anybody who turned up was then offered
a drink from the jug – cold stewed tea! It was absolutely foul.

These days you just don't appreciate just how tough times could be. When
I was a little girl we used to live upstairs in the house and there was a couple
living downstairs with two kids. One day the wife came up to ask if Mum would

like her to go and buy some cheese or something for her 'for thre'pence'. So Mum prodded and probed and eventually discovered the reason. Apparently the husband had finally got a job, but would have to go out very early the next morning to start work. The wife wanted to buy some tea, milk and sugar so that she could send him to work with a cup of tea inside him, and she quite literally didn't have a penny in the house. He would do the whole day's work on that cup of tea. Mum gave the woman sixpence to buy some lunch as well. Mum was like that. I can remember times when she sent me round to Mrs Somebody-or-other with a bag of potatoes, carrots and a few onions and the firm instruction that 'even if she offers, you must not take a penny for bringing it; not even a ha'penny!' She realised the woman was short and did something about it!

I will say this for Mum, whatever her many faults, she was generous and would not see anybody go hungry. And in those days people could go hungry and get into the most terrible state for the want of very little money. A couple of years after the war I was walking through Stratford and I met a girl I used to go to school with. After we had talked for a little while she said, 'Do you realise your mum saved my life?' I didn't, so she told me the story. Soon after we had left school she had to get married and they had one kid, but her husband couldn't get work and they just got deeper and deeper into poverty. Eventually they were just completely out of money, out of things to pawn, out of things to sell, and had borrowed as much as they could stand from friends and relatives. She had just had enough of the struggle and decided that she couldn't go on. So she was walking through Stratford trying to work out how to kill herself when she met Mum. They started talking and slowly the story came out about how desperate the family was. As they parted Mum gave her half-a-crown and that bought food for another day. After that, the mood of desperation passed and gradually things began to look up. As far as she was concerned, even looking back twenty years or so, she insisted that on that one day Mum saved her life for half-a-crown.

People were simply poor, and poor in a way you just don't see these days – and nor would you want to see it again. We were alright because Dad always had a job and was able to walk straight back into it after the war. That was leaving aside that because of his job he got us all the vegetables and fruit we wanted either free or cheap.

You could see barefoot children in the streets. Fred told me once that when he was in the senior class at school his teacher used to buy biscuits out of his own pocket and gave Fred the job of finding out who hadn't eaten any

Mary and Horatio Barker – the granpdarents – in about 1925.

breakfast before coming to school and giving them a biscuit each. It could be awful, but you just had to get by.

The Bacon family used to live a few doors from us when I was a girl. It was a second marriage for the wife, which was pretty unusual in those days, and from the way she spoke and acted I think she must have come down a lot. She was a bit classy, if the truth be told. That aside, though, they were ever so happy but very poor and so were always looking for ways to make money. Apart from anything else Mrs Bacon had a baby every year so it was a big family to feed and clothe. Anyway, I remember the time when they made a rag rug. These rugs were made by knotting together strips of rag in a particular sort of way and were very popular, I suppose they were cheap and nobody could afford carpets. Anyway, the Bacons sat round as a family and made this quite large rug. Then Mr Bacon went round the street selling tickets to raffle it. It was pretty good, well made and with good colours, so Mum showed a bit of interest. From then on she got the hard sell. He even cleared a space in front of the fire and showed her how good it looked. She agreed it looked good, but that was no help because she couldn't be sure of winning – at which Mr Bacon said he was sure she would win if she bought a ticket for five bob! Sure enough, she did win the rug, but she never took part in any more of the Bacons' money-making schemes because she didn't know who else had bought a ticket for five bob.

Life in the East End in the Depression wasn't easy, but we had our moments. I suppose in lots of ways we enjoyed even the simplest things more because they were so special and so unusual. The highlight of every year was Christmas and going to the Christmas pantomime. The rich people went on Boxing Day, because that was always a bit more expensive, but we used to go a day or so later. We always went to the Borough Theatre on the corner of Bridge Road – it was turned into a cinema later [Editor's note: the Rex]. The other theatres in Stratford were the Empire in the Broadway, but that was very posh and too expensive for us, and the Theatre Royal in Angel Lane [Editor's note: later the Theatre Royal, Stratford East, famous for Joan Littlewood's work], but that was too rough. The outing to the pantomime was a big event shared by all the neighbours. We always went to a matinee and us kids were sent up to the theatre to queue straight after breakfast. We would stay there all morning until lunchtime when the mums (and sometimes dads) would come up and bring sandwiches to eat. By the time we had eaten them the doors would open and in we would go. While the mums bought the tickets us kids had to run upstairs as fast as we could go to grab the right number of seats on the front row of the 'gods'. We would watch the show from there.

Because he was in the market, Dad didn't work on Mondays and so when I left school and started work he used to make my lunch for me on Monday mornings. He didn't have much idea really so there was nothing delicate about his lunches, but they were ever so welcome. He would just cut a couple of slices of bread and stick a quarter-pound of cheese between them, adding a cucumber from the market and anything else that came to hand. When I got to work I used to take the lunch apart again and share it out between those who were short. Sometimes three or four girls would share that lunch, and Monday became a high point of the week. As soon as I arrived at work girls would ask what 'dad' had given them for lunch today. It does doesn't bear thinking about, but that is how you live when things are really tight.

When Fred and I got married we took half a house, just up the road from Mum. In the downstairs half was a woman and her husband with five kids. Not only that, she had a brother who was out of work. He lived in one room a little distance away but spent a lot of time with the family (when he wasn't looking for work, that is) and always had Sunday dinner with them. The woman used to go out late on Saturday, when the meat was cheap – well, the butchers didn't have refrigerators like today so what they didn't sell on Saturday would be spoiled by Monday. The woman, her husband and her brother would then have the meat, whatever was cheap, for their dinner and the kids would have rabbit stew. Rabbit was always cheap. That was the only meat they ate all week, just on Sunday.

I remember one Monday though, when the woman came upstairs with a face like thunder, and clutching a bit of meat from the dustbin. My mum never had much idea with leftovers and always used to throw out anything that hadn't been eaten. I never really thought about it and just carried on the same. I suppose I thought that everybody did the same. Anyway, the woman suddenly stuck this piece of meat up in front of my face and asked, 'Did you throw this out?'

'Yes,' I muttered, 'we had too much.' I couldn't think what else to say.

'You are a wicked, evil, girl,' she said, 'Don't you realise there are kids in this house and you go throwing out perfectly good bits of meat.'

She really tore me off a strip and by the time she had finished with me I felt about half-an-inch tall. It had just never occurred to me to do anything else. Anyway, after that I always gave her any leftovers every Monday. In fact, I used to buy a little bit extra just to make sure of the leftovers. From then on, she and her husband used to save up thre'pence every week for half a pint of beer so that after the kids had gone to bed they would sit up and have meat sandwiches and beer. That was the highlight of the week for them.

6

Derby Day

(early 1920s)

My father was a porter in Stratford Market, then one of the most important fruit and vegetable markets in London. He was pretty good at it too and on one occasion he held the record for the number of baskets he could carry at one time. The fruit used to be packed in flat, circular, baskets which stacked on top of each other, and the porters used to carry them, piled-up, balanced on their heads. Of course it was hard work but it was steady and he was allowed a sack of vegetables every week as part of his pay.

Apart from the obvious holidays, like Christmas, Dad only got one day off a year and that was Derby Day. The whole market would close for the workers to have their day out to see the Derby. Dad, though, never went on the outing but instead used to go up to the Borough Market to see his old friends there. It was quite a day for him, and he used to get dressed up in his best suit for the highlight of his year. The only trouble was that Mum didn't trust him not to get thoroughly drunk, so to restrain him a bit each year she insisted that he took me along. It must have cramped his style, but I thought it was wonderful, because I too used to get dressed up in my best clothes and was taken off on an adventure up in London. We used to visit a succession of pubs and at each one he would disappear inside for varying lengths of time. I suppose he must have been a bit of a ladies' man in his time, because all the women used to make a tremendous fuss of him. Each one used to give him a great big kiss and wild exclamations of 'glad to see you Wally,' 'how are you Wally?' 'what's the news?' and so on.

Much more fun to me, though, was the fuss and attention that I got. Of course I had to stay outside the pub, or very occasionally I could stand just inside the door, but this endless succession of women would come out to see 'Wally's girl', ask me how I was, buy me a lemonade and sometimes give me a sixpence. I thought I was in heaven and could have stayed there forever. I could certainly drink as much lemonade as they could buy for me, it was wonderful.

I used to make a big profit on the day and, more to the point, I was allowed to keep it. On the bus home, Dad would ask me how much I had got and what did I want to do with it. Usually I would take a halfpenny a day to school and buy myself sweets on the way home. Just once, I bought a quarter of a pound of toffees and I sat on the wall round the corner from home, where nobody would see me, so that I could eat them all myself. Getting back to Derby Day, the most important question was then, did I have somewhere safe to keep the money I had collected? The answer to that was yes, the corner of my drawer. Dad would always finish by saying that 'Yes, that sounded alright,' but perhaps I should not tell my mother how much I had or where it had come from. I never needed to be told twice.

7

The Holy Cups

(about 1920)

Like all families in those days we more or less lived in the kitchen. Along one wall of the kitchen was a large dresser which was where all the kitchen hardware and that sort of stuff was stored. Up the back of the dresser were three shelves and these were used to store and display the china. On the bottom two shelves were the everyday bits and pieces, but the top shelf was Mum's pride and joy. There, carefully displayed, was the best china. I don't know where it had come from, maybe Grandma had bought it as a wedding present because she was quite well off by then, but it was clearly a class better than the rest. Of course, we never used it. In fact we never touched it, or even dared to touch it. It stood untouched and unmoved on the top shelf, just like a museum display.

Our house was the last but one in Carpenters Road. Beyond the next house, which was the last, there were factories all the way through to Hackney. One summer's day, and it must have been just after the war [Editor's note: First World War], Mum was standing on the doorstep watching the world go by. That was quite the usual thing to do then. Everybody used to leave their doors open and when you had time to spare you would stand in the doorway and chat to your neighbours up and down or across the street, and with anybody passing by. If you were particularly relaxed, or in the evening, you might even get a chair out and sit there.

Well, Mum was standing there when two nuns appeared coming down the road from the factory end. I suppose they had been round the factories on the scrounge for donations. Now Mum enjoyed a bit of religion – although Dad didn't. In fact he could be pretty brutal about it when he wanted to upset Mum. At Christmas, sometimes, he would express his views on the true nature of Jesus' parentage and 'virgin birth' in no uncertain, or delicate, terms. It used to send Mum off in a spin and I think she was genuinely worried that a thunderbolt would strike us all. I got the impression that Dad had seen too much suffering and death in the war to have time for any platitudes about peace and love. Anyway, Mum was always on for a spot of religion so when these nuns got nearer she greeted them with a most respectful 'Good afternoon, sisters.' They returned the greeting, and went on to ask if they might possibly have a drink of water. Mum got ever so excited and promptly invited them in for a cup of tea, which they graciously accepted.

When we got home from school we were immediately suspicious, because there on the table were two of the best cups and saucers from the top shelf. We couldn't believe it; we had thought that they would never, ever, come off the dresser. So Mum put on her most dignified voice and told us how the nuns had visited and sat at our table to drink a cup of tea. To be honest, we felt sorry for the nuns! Mum was a wonderful cook, she could cook anything even if she had never done it before, but there were three things she could not do: make jelly, make custard and make tea. You wouldn't have thought any of them were difficult, but they were beyond Mum. Her tea was undrinkable. It must have been a tribute to the nuns' Christian humility and charity, as well as desperation for a drink, that they sat at our table and drank her brew.

Now, of course, it was time to wash up. Normally we kids did all the washing up, but not the best china: that was far too precious. Mind you, even then she did the least she could without us kids actually touching the china. She sat at the table and called for a bowl of water – you always washed up in a bowl on the table, nobody ever used the sink. She called for an ordinary cup to collect the dregs in so that we could then pour them down the outside drain. She carefully emptied the first of her best cups into the dregs-cup, went white as a sheet, and exclaimed 'Oh my God!' She reached for the second cup, drained it just as carefully, looked into it and with a voice wobbling in emotion said again, 'Oh my God.' Then she sat back in the chair, and looked far away into the distance beyond the wall. We kids were stunned, then gathered the courage to look into the emptied cups. In the bottom of each was a collection of pins, needles, a razor blade, a thimble, buttons – all the things that you found laying around when you tidied up. Because the best china was never used Mum had got into the habit of dropping these odd bits and pieces into one of the cups whenever she came across them. She had been so excited about entertaining these nuns she hadn't thought to look into the cups as she poured the tea! Those poor nuns, to have to drink Mum's tea and then find the cups full of odds and sods – mostly sharp and dangerous ones. They must have wondered what sort of test was being given to their faith!

Of course, we kids thought it was hilarious. Nothing was ever said to Dad, but after that we always called the china on the top shelf 'The Holy Cups'.

8

The Prize

(about 1920)

We never had much money, especially when I was a little girl just after the First World War. I suppose we were lucky to have any money because there were plenty of people around us who had nothing at all, and I mean literally nothing at all. Anyway, one year I qualified to go away with the Ragged School Union Country Holiday Fund. This offered a week away in the country for just 10s. To be honest, I didn't want to go. I wasn't a very adventurous little girl and, I suppose, I was pretty insecure. I didn't want to leave Mum. But she said I would have to go, and how lucky I was to qualify, and how exciting it must be for me, until I thought I would have to go or there would be trouble. So I kept my mouth shut and just went.

The holiday was in a big house in Letchworth. I had no idea where Letchworth was; in fact I never came across it again until well after the Second World War. As far as a little girl from the East End of London was concerned it could have been anywhere – we were taken there in the back of a lorry, and by the time we arrived I could well believe it was on the other side of the world. I had never travelled so far in my life, I wasn't even sure you could travel 'so far' and still be in England.

We arrived in the late afternoon at this great big house just outside the town. As soon as we arrived we had to take a bath and a dose of Liquorice Powder to open the bowels. Maybe it was the excitement of the journey, maybe an attack of nerves, but my bowels remained firmly closed. The next morning, though, when I woke up I was absolutely bursting to go to the loo but that didn't matter to the 'powers' that were in charge. As soon as we got up the first task was to wash our hair and all my requests to go to the loo were ignored. According to their rules I couldn't possibly want the toilet at that time and that was the end of it. As they worked their way through us all doing our hair I got to feel worse and worse until I finally shouted out that I 'had to go!' The matron looked down at me for a couple of seconds, probably trying to make up her mind whether I was just trying to destroy their routine or whether I was afraid of having clean hair. Meanwhile, I could feel that my belly was on the verge of exploding. I had my legs wound tight together to try and contain the explosion until the last possible moment and was rocking my whole lower body backwards and forwards in a sort of desperate effort to encourage the muscles to hold together for a little bit longer. After looking at me for some time I think she had decided that I was being awkward and just wanted to get out of being clean, while getting a bit of attention at the same time. Her strategy must have been to humiliate me so as to teach me not to make a fuss. Instead of sending me off to the loo she said something to one of the staff who quickly went out through a door and reappeared a couple of moments later with a chamber pot. She put it down in front of me and matron 'invited' me to use it! To be honest, I didn't need any invitation. Normally I would have been terribly embarrassed and nothing would have made me use the loo in the presence of anybody else, but as soon as that pot touched the ground I had my knickers off and was on it. And my bowels just emptied and emptied and emptied. The stink was awful but I didn't care. At that moment I didn't have a care in the world, all I wanted to do was sit there and let my belly empty. Slowly the pain went off and my tummy relaxed. When I finally stood up the pot was full almost to the brim. In fact, it was so full they couldn't trust me to carry it away without spilling it. Instead, one of the staff got a cloth, which was carefully laid across the top of the pot, and it was carried ceremoniously away. The matron kept a very stiff upper lip and continued to look straight across the top of our heads, but I think it must have taken her aback. Especially when she thought how close she had been to disaster.

I can't remember much about the holiday. Its most lasting legacy came from having porridge for breakfast every day – I have disliked porridge ever since. Apart from that, I think that most days we used to play games in the grounds. But one day we were going into the town to look at the shops and maybe buy presents for our families. As it happened, every lunchtime from school I used to go and get half a pint of beer for an old lady who lived up the street and she would give me sixpence a week. She had fallen behind with my 'pay' and eventually one of her daughters gave me a postal order for 2s 6d just before the holiday so I was really rich. But before I could get any presents I had to cash this postal order, and the matron decided I should go to town with her for the purpose. All the other kids wanted to come with us, but matron refused. That morning we got up and had breakfast as usual but we had to wash 'especially clean' and were then lined up to walk into town. Except the matron called me to one side and told me to wait. I kicked up one hell of a fuss, but she wouldn't change her mind, and I had to stand there as all the others trailed off in a long crocodile towards the town.

I was decidedly upset and decidedly suspicious. Then things got worse, because matron told me to go and put on my Sunday best. Well, Sunday best was exactly that; you did not dare to wear it at any other time, Mum would have killed you! So again I kicked up merry hell and said how you could not wear Sunday best on any other day, Mum would get ever so cross, it wasn't right and all the rest, but it didn't help. In the end I had to go off to get changed into my best mauve and white! I was a reasonably pretty child and in good clothes must have looked quite presentable.

When I got back downstairs to the hall matron was already there, dressed up to the nines with a very impressive hat on the top. I was getting more and more worried by the minute – after all, I hadn't wanted to leave my Mum in the first place and now we were getting all dressed up on the wrong day.

'Come on then Mary,' she said, 'we are going into town.' That was exactly what we did, following the steps all the others had taken half an hour earlier. Goodness knows what was wrong with the woman, I guess these days she would be sent for counselling, but everywhere we went she introduced me as her daughter. Whether it was just her fantasy, or whether she had had a husband and daughter who had died, or whatever was going on, I just do not know. I am sure none of the people we met were at all fooled: you couldn't keep secrets in little places like that. As far as I was concerned, though, it was terribly worrying because I was not her daughter and I didn't want to be her daughter. My Mum was back home, and that was where I wanted to be.

Of course, by then the other kids had seen us and were tagging along to see what was going on. That gave me some comfort, so I tried to keep them with us. We went into all sorts of shops, some of which we kids would never have gone into on our own. The other kids thought it was marvellous that I was going in and started asking me to buy things. Since I wanted to keep them with us I obliged with whatever they wanted – including loads of bananas which most of the kids had never tasted before. I spent pretty well all my money in the process, but it was worth it. I think matron was showing me off around the town and giving everybody the story about me being her daughter. It was a tremendous relief to get back to the house and be able to dress in my ordinary clothes and start playing with everybody else again.

Back at school we had to write an essay, well in those days we called it a 'composition', about the holiday. You can guess that the idea terrified me and I couldn't possibly tell the truth about it and how I had felt. I couldn't think what to say. However, all the grown-ups had gone on and on about what a wonderful opportunity it was, how beautiful it was in the country, the trees and the walks, all the fun and games we would enjoy with each other as children, how dedicated the staff were and how good the food was and so on, so I decided that the best thing was to repeat it all. That is what I did, working in everything that 'they' had said and not revealing any of my own feelings and terrors. The big surprise was many weeks later when I was called to the governess' room to be told that I had won the essay prize for my age group. The school was very proud of me and greatly honoured by the prize, so they wanted me to go up to the Mansion House in London to receive my prize, and would my parents be able to take me up there on the appointed Saturday? Honestly, I had been doing my best to forget about the whole thing; I had hated the holiday and believed that I had come within a hair's breadth of never going home ever again. Suddenly it had come back to haunt me. So I looked very sad and told the governess that my parents couldn't possibly take me to collect the prize. She tut-tutted and said she quite understood, though really she didn't have the faintest idea. Another narrow escape, or so I thought.

Two days later she sent for me again. This time she told me that the school was so honoured, and they so wanted me not to be disappointed, that Miss Davidson would give up her Saturday afternoon to take me to the prize-giving. There was no way out of this so I finally gave in and accepted the inevitable. She gave me a letter for my parents explaining the arrangements and that Miss Davidson would meet me at the tram stop in the High Road at whatever time it was. Mind you, when it came to it Mum and Dad were ever so proud of me and when I got home I had a terrible job explaining to them why a teacher had to take me and they couldn't go! Really, telling lies is not worth the hassle, you have to be so quick-witted and have such a good memory about what you have already said, and even then each lie just gets you into more complications.

Come the fateful Saturday I got all dressed up in my Sunday best, in fact Mum bought me a new Sunday dress. It was bottle green, I remember. I got dressed up in that, shoes and stockings, and my best hat. Mum was so proud of me I had to be dragged in next door to show off to Mrs Nicholson, and then I sat watching the clock waiting for the dreaded time to come round. Dad worked on Saturday mornings and always stopped in the pub for a couple of drinks with his mates on the way home. Just before I was due to go out he came in, drunk as usual. He looked at me approvingly and said how nice I looked, but then said he wasn't so sure about the arrangements. He had stopped in at the Greengate pub as usual when Miss Davidson had come in so he had got talking to her. He was shocked, he said, by her language and the way she swore – her being an educated lady, too. Even worse was the way she drank, not beer but shorts. She could put down the whisky faster than he was drinking his beer. He had to admit that she had drunk him under the table, and there were not many men who could do that let alone a Miss Schoolteacher. My eyes were popping out of my head and I was ashamed, scared, humiliated, and shocked, all at the same time.

'Did you say you were my dad?' I sort of asked.

'Of course,' he replied and went off on an even more lurid account of Miss Davidson and her drinking. Mum didn't seem at all worried and suddenly said it was time to go, and packed me off on my way.

I couldn't understand why Mum was so relaxed about it all and so I walked up to the High Road going slower and slower, wondering whether I could run away somewhere. When I reached the end of the road there was Miss Davidson standing at the tram stop and waving to me, so there was nothing more to be done. We waited for the tram in silence and when it came we went upstairs. I was absolutely terrified about what had happened and what Miss would say, but she seemed to ignore everything that had gone before. When she spoke I carefully tried to smell her breath but couldn't pick up any hint of alcohol, which just proved to me that all Dad had said about her being a hardened drinker must be true. How else could she cover up so well?

We got to the Mansion House and I was led off with the prize-winners while Miss went off to the audience seats. I don't recall much about the actual prize-giving, or the rest of the day. My prize was a picture of a dog – or it might have been a puppy. Mum was ever so proud of it that she had it framed (without glass!) and it went on display on the mantelpiece. It stayed there until I got married and moved out. At first I just wanted to forget the whole affair but it wasn't possible with the picture stuck there in front of me. After a while

I began to like the picture and, I suppose, feel a bit proud of myself. We kept it right until we were bombed out. When the salvage workers were struggling to see what they could save I told them not to bother with the picture; after all, there were much more pressing issues. Looking back, I think it would have been nice to have salvaged it, but it is too late now.

After the war, a long time after the war, I had a sudden rush of revelation. The pub at the tram stop was what we used to call a beer pub. It just had a couple of pumps of beer on draught and a couple of types of bottled beer and that was it – it never sold spirits. No wonder Mum was so relaxed about Dad's lurid tale of Miss Davidson's drinking.

9

A Daughter's Story

(about 1925)

In the early 1950s I got an early morning job cleaning the offices of a factory up near Bow. Somehow I seemed to meet all sorts in that job and some of them were really odd. They would tell you stories that just didn't and couldn't make sense – it used to leave me dumbstruck that they expected you to believe them, but I listened anyway. If nothing else, it helped the job go along. I do remember the story of one young woman though – it still makes me shudder to think about the Depression and what happened to people.

This young woman came to work as a cleaner for a while. She was ever so nice, quiet and easy going, and never had a cross word for anyone. Until, that is, one morning when three or four of us were working at one end of the Drawing Office and she was at the other. One of the women with us put on a disapproving face, gestured down to the other end and said that 'she got sent for again last night' and went on to tell us, in a stage whisper, about 'her mother, always drunk,' and how she would 'have to keep going down the pub to collect her.' She was just getting into her stride when the young woman reacted. She came storming down from the other end of the office, her lips pulled in so tight that it looked as though if her mouth opened there would be an explosion. She fixed us all in one stare that had us rooted to the spot. Finally she spoke, 'My mum's welcome to get drunk any time she wants to. And they can send for me to collect her any time of the day or night. And she'll have a home wherever I am for as long as she needs it or wants it.' And then she told us her story.

Her mum had got married just after the First World War and soon had two daughters – this woman was the older of them – followed a few years later by a son. It wasn't easy, well life wasn't easy for anyone then, but they managed and were getting along as well as anybody else around Stratford. They were living in two rooms at the time, nothing like luxury but at least it was home. Then the husband died. Within a week or so the tiny savings were gone, the rent wasn't paid, and they were simply thrown out onto the streets. That was it, a young woman with two daughters aged about six or seven and a baby son, with nowhere to live. Their only possessions were a couple of bits of clothes apiece and the bucket, scrubbing brush, soap, stone and apron that her mum had salvaged from their home.

Luckily it was summer, so they walked over to Victoria Park and just used to wander around there. The two girls would look after the baby in one of the shelters that dotted the park and their mum would go off round the streets, knocking on doors to get work scrubbing steps and the like. With the couple of coppers she made from this she would buy food and return to the shelter in the park to spend the night with the kids. That was how they lived for the rest of the summer. It couldn't last, though, and as the year wore on it got colder and colder until eventually the winter meant that they just had to find some proper shelter.

Well, her mother had a brother who lived over in Poplar so she and the kids walked over there. There was nothing he could do. If he had taken them in he would have been in trouble with the landlord and soon been on the streets himself. Maybe he didn't want to do anything, I don't know. Anyway, the best he could, or maybe would, do was to let the family sleep in his hall. They couldn't come in until it was getting dark and would bed down straight away on the floor. The brother would lend them a blanket but that wasn't much between the four of them, and with no heating it was bitterly cold. Then next morning, almost as soon as it was light, they would have to go out again and spend the day on the streets. As before, they would find whatever shelter they could and the girls would look after the baby while their mum did whatever work she could find.

It couldn't last. The end came when they woke up one morning and found that the little boy had died of cold during the night. Of course, then the story came out and there was a dreadful scandal – it was a pity nobody thought of that when the family had been thrown out onto the streets in the first place.

A shelter in Victoria Park, possibly the one the girl's family had to sleep in over the summer. © Patricia Philpott, English Heritage/ National Monument Record

Anyway, the mum was forced into the workhouse and the two girls put into a home.

Despite all that had happened she was determined to keep her family together and she kept in touch with the two girls, visiting regularly and promising that they would get back together again. She managed to get a job and then rent a couple of rooms and when the older girl was thirteen, her mum was able to get her out of the home. They both got jobs and eventually got the other daughter out when she was fourteen. While she had been in the home she had learned to speak ever so posh so that when she came out she used to get into all sorts of trouble because people thought she was putting it on and trying to show them up. In the end the older girl had to get a job in the same place as the younger one just so she could look after her and keep her out of trouble!

Anyway, that was it. Slowly they got back on their feet, managed to get a little house and build a home, the daughters got married and in the end the mum went to live with our 'young woman'. That was her story, but she finished it by repeating where she had started; 'Mum is welcome to get drunk any time she likes and she will always have a home with me!'

10

The B Family

(1920–7)

When I was a girl my best friend was Jenny B. She was one of a large family, with one sister and goodness knows how many brothers – loads and loads of them. Us kids and the Bs were all the same sort of ages, and so we all played with each other. Although the rest of them just played, me and Jenny 'clicked' and we became very close friends until the passage of time took us on different paths. I must say that Jenny was not at all good looking, in fact she looked a bit funny. But she had the most wonderful nature and she was the nicest person you could ever know.

The family were all clever enough and did well. I think Jenny was the brightest; she and I were the only ones from our school to get the scholarship and both of us could have gone to the grammar school, but neither of us was allowed to. I seem to remember that the second brother was a bit simple – not the full two bob – but he was a real hard worker. He would have a go at anything and really put his back into it. In fact, he always managed somehow or other and in time got married, had a family, and for as long as I heard about him was ever so happy. The youngest brother was Tommy, who was about the same age as our Bob. Mr B had been badly wounded in the war and, although he survived it somehow, he was never well and never worked again. In fact he only survived a couple of years and died soon after the war, from his wounds if the truth be told. I think it was because of this that the British Legion took an interest in the family and they more or less took Tommy over. We only heard the occasional bit of news, but did hear that he had gone to university. I don't think we had any idea what that really meant, but it sounded good.

Another of my brother's friends was Ginger. He had a rough life, poor kid. His mother was suicidal and every so often she would have to be pulled out of the canal and taken back home. I suppose nowadays she would be given some help or something but there was nothing like that then. Anyway, as you can guess, Ginger had the biggest mop of ginger hair that you had ever seen. The other thing about Ginger, though, was that he was incredibly tall. He was only a kid like the rest of us, but he was already as big or bigger than most adults. The trouble was, he was as clumsy as any other kid, maybe worse because of his size. Mum used to fly into a real panic whenever he called round for the boys – 'tell him to be careful,' 'don't go there,' 'hurry up and get him outside' – anything to get him out of the house. She was absolutely terrified that he would walk into one of the gas mantles. We had gas lights in those days and the mantles were extremely expensive and unbelievably fragile. You only had to touch them and they would disintegrate, and the sight of Ginger's enormous frame trying to fit into our house was more than Mum could stand. Maybe he had already broken one of the mantles but I don't remember it at all.

During the Second World War he was called up and went in the army. I am not sure whether it was in the desert or Normandy, but he was terribly wounded in some battle. He said himself he could feel that he was dying and slowly slipping away, when he heard this really brutal voice suddenly shout at him, 'Right you ginger bastard, don't die on me now!' He said that he was so shocked he could feel himself struggle to get control again and open his eyes. When he did, he looked up and found himself looking straight at Tommy B. He had become a doctor and was in the Medical Corps. He was as surprised as anybody to find a 'dying' friend from his childhood on the battlefield, but Ginger was convinced that Tommy had pulled him back from death and saved his life.

After the war Tommy returned to Stratford and worked at the London Hospital. He never married, but lived with the eldest of his brothers who was a writer and artist. Sadly he died quite young – he got appendicitis but being a doctor didn't take proper notice of it and by the time they operated it was too late. He was very well known and much loved around Stratford and the whole place came to a stop for his funeral.

Going back to Jenny, we were great friends all through school and even when we started work. Then she sort of disappeared in a bit of a scandal. There was a lady up the road who was the local 'unofficial' midwife. She was not trained at all, but had lots of experience and had delivered most of the babies in the street; certainly those of the poorer families who couldn't afford to go to the hospital. She knew what she was doing. Anyway, one day she was visiting the Bs and there were several people around when Jenny came in. Without thinking, she asked, 'Oh, and when are you going to have the baby then?' Goodness knows what, but she instantly recognised from her body shape or something that Jenny was pregnant. The family had managed to cover it up until then and nobody in the street had suspected anything, but now the cat was out of the bag. There was a terrible stink and Mum went mad and said I was never to talk to Jenny again. It didn't matter because, as I said, Jenny more or less disappeared. It turned out that the father was a married man. Believe it or not, he was married to the local Stratford Beauty Queen but somehow he got caught up with Jenny for all her funny looks. He left his wife and set up home with Jenny and they did, like the fairy story, live happily ever after.

I know that because years after the war we were going out to a dinner and, as we were walking into the station dressed up to the nines, we came face to face with Jenny. I don't know who was most surprised but we had a rapid catch-up on twenty years or more. To be honest, I would have rather sat on the platform all night and carried on talking, but we had paid for the tickets and it was important to my husband Fred so we went to the dinner. She was a lovely girl.

11

Families

(1925)

When I look back I can see that we had a pretty good life really. Dad was always in work and because of his work in the market we always had plenty of food. He used to drink a lot – somehow it seemed to be part of life in the market – and almost always came home drunk or, at least, 'the worse for wear', but family came first and he always gave Mum her money. He only ever came home stone cold sober once that I can remember and that was from the funeral of a friend who also worked in the market. He had only been a young man, younger than Dad, but one day he suddenly dropped dead at work. It affected all his mates, including Dad, pretty badly. On the day of the funeral Dad got dressed up in all his best clothes – and he could be an extremely smart man – went out and not much more than an hour later was back again without having had a single drink. He walked into the house, sober and absolutely immaculate. The dog took one look at him, growled and bit him. He had never seen 'this man' before and didn't recognise him, so assumed he was an intruder!

I had no complaints though. Dad looked after his family and we always had a home there. There was a fellow round the corner who reckoned to look after his kids until they were 'old enough' and then they were turned out. 'Old enough' to him meant fifteen, and he was absolutely rigid about it with no exceptions. I suppose he had to be because there was never any spare room in their house. They had a new baby every year without fail, the last one when his wife was fifty-seven! That must be a bit of a record in itself.

One day the mother came round to see Mum to ask whether she could give the latest leaver, a daughter, a home. She was ever so worried because this daughter was partially crippled and her mother couldn't see how she could possibly manage. The daughter had fallen off a roundabout in the park when she was a child and had broken her leg. The medical services weren't so good in those days and she had ended up with one leg shorter than the other. That still didn't alter her father's rules – she was fifteen and had to stand on her own (crippled) feet. Anyway there were six of us kids, as well as Mum and Dad, in our three-bedroom house so it was out of the question for her to come to us. In desperation she went to live with her boyfriend's family and, sure enough, a few months later they had to get married.

Several years later when I was expecting my first boy, I was at the hospital maternity clinic waiting to be examined. Suddenly this voice boomed out from the nurse on duty, 'Oh no, not you again, you have not paid for the last two yet!' In those days you had to pay to go to hospital, and that included having babies, but I suppose this woman was just too poor. Of course, we all peered round the end of the waiting room to see what was going on and there was the crippled girl, a lot older by then of course. I do not know what she did in the end but she was never at the clinic again when I was there. I suppose she must have managed somehow.

She had quite a large family in the end, and they all made something of themselves. I cannot remember what they did, but they all got good jobs and made good money, which is pretty remarkable when you think what an unpromising start in life they all had. That said, the eldest child was a daughter, who made a speciality of going out with other women's husbands! She was totally unashamed about it, and if any of the wives ever objected she told them in no uncertain terms that they ought to be grateful. Firstly, they knew where their husbands were and secondly she was clean and so they would not come to any harm! They could, she always maintained, do a lot worse on both counts.

12

The Goose

(1921)

Mum had a lot of faults, but you couldn't fault her cooking. She really was an excellent cook, even if everybody else had to run round after her doing all the odd jobs: washing up, fetching and carrying and so on. She had a real instinct for food, and could usually make a good job of something even if she had never cooked it before. Mind you, when the food was cooked she really couldn't serve it up sensibly and you got the most odd portions. If she shared out a pie the first couple of slices would be enormous and then they would get smaller and smaller until the last person got what was left!

About the only exception to her 'instinct for food' was Weetabix. We usually had a cooked meal for breakfast – eggs, bacon, a kipper, even a piece of steak sometimes. I suppose we ate very well really. Against that, she would never serve up cereals. In her book 'oats were for horses!' Anyway, when this wonderful new cereal came out and everybody was talking about it she decided to give it a try. It never occurred to her to read the instructions and instead she set about it the same way as porridge – after all, that was how you cooked cereals. First she put a pint of milk on to boil and to it added the whole box of Weetabix. Needless to say, the liquid was almost instantly soaked up, so she had to add more, and more, and then put it in a bigger saucepan, and so on until she had an enormous saucepan of bubbling brown porridge. By then she had rumbled that something had gone wrong, but that didn't deter her. Above all she wouldn't allow any waste, so we kids had to eat the lot. But we never had it again – and all she ever said about it was 'new fangled bloody cereals'.

One Christmas a customer at the market gave Dad a goose as a present. We always used to have chicken at Christmas, you never saw turkey then. But this Christmas Dad proudly announced that he had a goose and that would be our dinner – Mum did her nut, she didn't know how to cook the thing so 'what's the bloody point of that?' she asked. Nothing would deter Dad, though.

The goose, when it arrived, looked like the largest goose in the world, not that we had any idea how big a goose should be. Mum took one look at it and started up all over again – it was too big to fit in the oven, it was too big to fit in the dustbin, it was even too big to bury in our backyard (our backyard was no bigger than a postage stamp!), she didn't know what to do with it, it was a silly idea, Dad could cook the bloody thing himself, and on and on and on. Dad did the only sensible thing and went off to the pub leaving Mum and us children to set about the goose. It barely fitted in the roasting tray, in fact it sat on the tray rather than in it. Having no idea what goose was like she decided to play safe, so first she liberally spread it with cooking fat, just in case it went dry, and then added some fat bacon to help keep it moist.

Now, the back room downstairs was our kitchen, living and dining room, the whole lot. Really we lived in that room. The cooking was done on the kitchener, a sort of range, which heated the room too. When the goose was ready she took it over to the oven but there was no way it could possibly fit in. Mind you, she tried. Put it this way and that, pulled it, pushed it, swore at it but nothing worked. We were getting desperate but it didn't worry Mum.

At the back of the kitchen was a little scullery and this had a gas oven. I don't think it had ever been used before but this was its moment. Mind you, the first thing Mum did was to send me out to clean it. It was thick with rust and dirt and I spent ages scraping and scrubbing. Eventually it was alright, or at least all the loose rust and dirt had been removed though it still looked pretty unsavoury. Even so, the goose still didn't fit. Then Mum came up with her master-stroke. In the roof of the oven was a small hook. Goodness knows what it was supposed to be used for, but Mum used some string to tie the goose up with its backside in the air and hung it from the hook. No roasting dish or anything like that, just the goose hanging up with its neck on the floor of the oven and its backside pressed against the hook, held in place by string. She lit the gas and we all retreated back to the kitchen.

About an hour or so later somebody went out into the scullery, I think they were going through into the backyard (the loo was out there) and let out the most enormous scream.

'Quick, quick, the oven's leaking! There's water pouring all over the floor!' We all rushed out and sure enough there was a steady stream of clear liquid dripping out of the oven door and onto the floor. Of course, it was fat. Geese are most dreadfully fatty creatures and Mum had piled goodness knows how much extra fat on top of it. We were all horror-struck, and had visions of no Christmas dinner but Mum was totally unimpressed.

'Go and get some sacks from under the stairs' she ordered. Part of Dad's pay in the market was a free load of vegetables every week – it was called his 'cochel', goodness knows where the word came from – and he used a sack to bring them home. The sacks had to be returned but he used to collect half a dozen or so and then take them back in one go. Anyway, we grabbed his collection of sacks and laid them all over the scullery floor. Then we retreated again to the kitchen and got on with the rest of dinner.

As I said earlier, Mum was a good cook and so, as usual, it was a gorgeous dinner (as long as you didn't think of the state of the oven it was cooked in). After dinner Mum and Dad went to sleep, the other kids were sent off visiting, and I was detailed to do the washing up. When I went into the scullery the mess was awful. The fat had soaked into the sacking, people had been paddling in and out of it and then it had set solid. I was only a little kid and I had no idea what to do, so I woke up Mum. She wasn't very happy about it but just fumed into the kitchen, picked up the sacks as they were and stuffed them into the dustbin. And that was that, except that nobody ever dared to mention goose in the house from that day forward.

Well, that is not quite true. The postscript came some years later when I was going out with Fred. He won a goose in a raffle at work or something. One evening he came to see me, all happy and bright, told us of his fortune, and presented his winnings to Mum. Everybody in the house went silent. We all froze in terror, and waited . . . Mum just smiled, said how generous he was and thanked him most extravagantly.

13

Working Life

(1925–54)

Iremember starting work. I lay awake all through the night before praying.
I was so scared. Of course, it was no problem and all of us had to do it, but
I still remember the feeling. We left school at fourteen then so really I was
only a kid at the time. We wouldn't dream of sending kids out at that age now.
Still, I suppose times change.

My birthday came in August, which made me pretty young in my class.
Because of the way the rules worked I had to go back to school after the
summer holidays and I then left at the end of September. There were several
of us due to leave and one morning, in assembly, it was announced that 'All
those leaving on the thirtieth of September must go to see the governess.' We
all trooped down to her room and lined up, then we were called in all together
and lined up in front of her.

'I have been told,' she said 'that Clarnico wish to take on a number of
school leavers. You should all go along there and you may have time out from
school for this purpose.' Clarnico was a rather high-class sweet factory over at
Hackney, about 2 miles away. It was quite a walk but I suppose we didn't think
anything about it – in those days you walked everywhere.

Anyway, off we all went. I think I must have gone home and Mum let me put
on my Sunday dress, stockings and shoes. I was walking with Jenny because
we were big friends. Suddenly she stopped walking and burst into tears. When

I finally got her to speak she said that she couldn't possibly get a job if she didn't have coloured stockings. She only had the same 'horrible old black ones' that all of us had! She was in such a state over it, though, that I dug out all the money I had – it was thre'pence – and she added all hers to it – another three ha'pence – and we went into the drapers and bought her a pair of coloured stockings. She put them on under the arch of Carpenters Road railway bridge – I will always remember that. Coloured stockings had only just come in and they caused a terrible stir. I can remember Dad standing at the top of our stairs screaming to my mother at the top of his voice to 'get her in, she hasn't got anything on.' From the top of our stairs you could see down through the open door into the street. And there was my older sister standing in the street feeling ever so fashionable in her pink stockings.

'If you want her in, you get her in,' replied Mum, 'and she has got stockings on.' Dad was really scandalised though and kicked up a terrible fuss. It took ages for the atmosphere to cool down again.

Anyway, we got down to Clarnico and went to the office. We sat there for a bit and then were shown down to the canteen. After a bit this very smart man came in and spoke to us. He was terribly smart, wearing a suit and a tie, with a real upper class accent. Goodness knows what he saw when he looked at us because we were a raggedy, untidy bunch. I can't remember what he said, but they took us all on. That is how I got my first job. I left school on the Friday afternoon and started work the following Monday morning, for 10s a week.

My first job was carrying trays of caramel up three flights of stairs. They must have been 2ft or more and weighed a ton – I could barely lift them. Goodness knows why they put me on the job because I was a skinny little thing then, there wasn't anything of me. You wouldn't let a kid do it these days, not any kid, but we didn't think about it – it was a job. Still, that is what I did all day every day. Looking back I feel as though I was on that for about three years, but that doesn't make much sense. The caramels and boxes of chocolates were for the Christmas trade, so that used to slacken off during October as the shops got their stock in. People then used to get moved over onto other things, the next big job being Easter eggs. For some reason, though, when I went over to chocolate they put me into 'Enrobing', that is, working the machines that coated the various centres with chocolate. It was very hot in there, I suppose the chocolate had to be kept warm while it was melted, but I enjoyed the work. I learned lots of jobs in that department. I got to be very good at marking the chocolates; making the squiggles on the tops that tell you what they are in the box. We used to have a pot of hot chocolate beside us and using either a finger or a stick had to pick up a blob of chocolate and make the design on each chocolate as it went by on the conveyor belt. It wasn't hard work, but you had to be ever so quick. The other big job was packing. It was amazing how quick you could get at assembling a box (they came ready glued but flattened), picking out the right chocolates and putting them in the box. We used to do that from eight in the morning until five-thirty, with just an hour for lunch and no tea break or anything like that. Mind you, I was very good at it and also made some good friends. That was where I met Daisy, and we stayed the closest of friends for the rest of our lives, or rather, her life.

One year, though, there was just not enough work and we got laid off. It was like that then, things were difficult and if there was no work you got laid off. I went down to the Labour [exchange] and they said that there were jobs up at Whitfields. That was a sweet factory just round the corner from the Greengate (a pub in the south of the borough). It was a terrible place, especially after Clarnico. I suppose Clarnico was a high-class firm making high-class chocolates, but not this place. It was dirty and tacky, and you never wanted to eat any of their sweets after you had worked there. I remember that when we arrived we had to wait in this big room and eventually a woman came out and said they wanted packers, 'was there anybody with experience?' she asked. Well, I had plenty of experience so I put my hand up, and so did this young woman standing beside me. As we were following the woman through the factory the other young woman asked in a whisper if I knew anything about packing.

'Well, of course,' I replied. The truth is that I didn't have the wit to lie about such a thing.

'Do you mind if I work with you then?' she asked, 'only I don't know anything but I am absolutely desperate for the job so I lied.' So she worked with me, and soon learnt. That lunchtime she asked where I was going to eat. There wasn't much I could do really because it was far too far away for me to go home. So she invited me to go home with her for lunch, she only lived around the corner. From then on I used to go there every lunchtime.

I didn't work there for very long though, thank heavens. It really was a dirty place and not at all up to the standards I was used to. It seems as though things picked up and Clarnico called me back. I wasn't sure what I should do because I had never left anywhere before, 'they' had always laid me off! I decided to be dreadfully secretive and just said, as officially as I could make it sound, that I wouldn't be back tomorrow. It didn't seem to bother them at all. I suppose workers for that sort of job were easy to come by. So I went back to Clarnico and to working with Daisy again. They put us in 'Fancy Goods', wrapping all sorts of speciality lines. Daisy and I made a good team, we just worked ever so well together and seemed to do even better together than either of us alone. I think it must have established a bit of a reputation for us.

During one of the lay-off periods Fred and I got married and that was the end of work. For a start, the firm insisted that you left – somehow they were unhappy about married women, perhaps they were worried about competition from home. Then there was a sort of social argument – if you had a husband you had somebody to feed you and jobs should go to the poor devils who had to feed themselves. Nobody ever said this, but it was understood by everybody. Lastly, Fred was totally against the idea of me working; he really thought it was below his dignity for his wife to work. He never did like the idea of me working and was never a bit helpful. He wouldn't even get his own breakfast and if he was ever in from work before me wouldn't put things on to cook, even if I had prepared them all. Mind you, he was happy enough with the extras that the money eventually bought.

When any young woman left Clarnico to get married she always got a £5 gratuity from the firm. I had got married during a lay-off, but Daisy said that we should go down and try it on them anyway. I was ever so scared but she egged me on and down we went. We went to the personnel department and they gave me a form which I filled out and gave back to them. Then they said to wait, so I waited, and suddenly there was my £5. Now £5 was real money, I had never seen that much in my life. We bought our first radio with it. That was the first 'extra' that we ever had and it made us ever so posh: I think we were the first people to have a radio in the whole street.

A little while later it was coming towards the Christmas rush time and Daisy said that she thought we ought to go down and see whether Clarnico would take us on even though we were not single. I didn't think it could possibly be worth the effort, because they just never took on married women. But Daisy kept on and on, so in the end we went down there and to my amazement they took us on. I suppose things were beginning to get a little bit better and they couldn't just pick up youngsters as and when they wanted them. From then on I stayed full-time right up to the war. Because of our experience we went straight into 'Fancy Goods', packing all their special lines through the year. Really we had a wonderful time and did incredibly well out of it. We got staff discount on everything we bought and I had plenty of money in my pocket. I used to buy sweets for all the kids in the street sometimes, and always at Christmas. One Easter we did chocolate eggs with children's names written on them, so I got them for a lot of the kids. They used to think I was marvellous and I was ever so popular – you can imagine. I got things for us as well. One year they did a Father Christmas figure whose top lifted off and inside was filled with 'mystery gifts' attached to trailing ribbons, blue for men and pink for women. We kept that for years – in fact I think it survived the war – and used to get it out and repack it every Christmas.

I suppose Clarnico were, for their time, really good employers. Another of their schemes was a yearly bonus for workers. I can't remember what you had to do to qualify, but they used to make a great performance out of it. They used to hire the Peoples Palace up the Mile End Road for the occasion and we all had to troop up there to collect our money. The Clarnico band was there to play music all the way through the ceremony and all the managers would be sat up on the platform. Then we would line up and file past one at a time to be given our brown envelope with the bonus inside. One time I got a £5 note and it caused a real stir – nobody in our street had ever seen one before and nobody would change it for me. In the end my Mum went down to the corner shop and told them that if they didn't change it she would never shop there again. So they changed it – but they also 'exhibited' it in the window for a couple of days! It's a wonder it didn't get pinched.

Even though he enjoyed the money, Fred hated the idea of me working but had to put up with it. Because of the extra money we were able to move to a flat in Manor Park. That was proper upmarket then – 'frightfully, frightfully' high class. Fred really enjoyed that: as I said, he was a right social climber. Not that I should complain about him because he gave me a good life. He was a compulsive 'joiner' but couldn't join anything without working away until he ran it, and I got all the benefit of the social life that went with it. He was a big wheel in the Swimming Club (local and county), the Freemasons, the Buffaloes and goodness knows what else in his time. Even when he retired and took a part-time kitchen job up in a London Gentlemen's Dining Club within six months he had his own set of keys, was in charge of the silverware, and was virtually assistant kitchen/cellar manager for their formal dinners.

Looking back to where he came from, from the very worst bit of Stratford which was itself a pretty rough part of the East End, he made a great deal of himself and in his quiet way was proud of it. He once said to me that there couldn't be many people from his background who had made a speech to a banquet in the Connaught Rooms, up in the City. And he was right. He was a climber, and was proud of himself, but he always said that his proudest moment was at some formal dinner or other, when he was being installed as President of whatever it was, and in his introduction the Chairman congratulated him that his son had just got a place at Cambridge. He admitted to crying in public for about the only time in his life!

Anyway, back to Manor Park. We lived there for a couple of years but then my aunt announced she had found us a 'nice house' in Keogh Road, back in Stratford. It must have been early 1940. My aunt was full of praises for this house though I think its main attraction was that it was next door to her. Uncle was ill and was getting progressively worse so that he had to go to hospital every couple of weeks. I think she just wanted somebody 'family' next door to help look after him. One Saturday we arranged to go over to have a look at the house, though I didn't feel much like it. In fact I felt decidedly off colour and distinctly sick but I had promised Aunty that I would look. She was right, it was a nice little house and Keogh Road was much the better end of Stratford.

Being as I was nearby I decided that I might as well visit Mum while I was at it. By the time I got there I was feeling really ill. I knocked on her door and as soon as she opened it I didn't say a word but rushed straight past and into the loo to be sick. When I felt better I started telling her the story, about looking at the house but not feeling too good and so on and so on. She didn't say a word until she looked me in the eye and asked, 'are you carrying then?' It just hadn't occurred to me up until then. We had been married for years, never taken any precautions but nothing had ever happened so I had just put such things out of my mind. Anyway, I was carrying so that was the end of my career in Clarnico and also made the decision to take the house.

I didn't go back to work until the early 1950s when both boys were at school and I got fed up with being at home all day. I saw an early morning office-cleaning job advertised in the local paper and to me it seemed ideal. It meant the boys would have to get themselves off to school in the morning, but I could be home by soon after nine so I was there pretty well all day in the holidays or if they were off school for any reason. I didn't say anything to Fred until after I got the job, because I knew he would object. He did object; in fact he never approved and never cooperated with anything to make my working life easier. Even so, the job suited me, suited the family and I enjoyed it, so I stayed there until we moved away from London in the mid-1960s.

14

Meeting and Marrying Fred
(1929–32)

As mentioned, Mum, Dad and us seven children lived upstairs in half a house in Lett Road. Downstairs lived the Ms, including their son Frank. Looking back, I think that he quite fancied me, but I was too innocent to notice. Mum noticed though, and was forever warning me about him, about being careful, about keeping away from him. I honestly didn't know what she was talking about – I must have been pretty naïve. Anyway, he was part of a group of friends that included Fred. Looking back on it they must have been a real bunch of tearaways but I never saw them in that sort of way at the time – I suppose youngsters never do. They used to go round to each other's houses so I saw quite a lot of them, including Fred.

One day they went swimming at the baths in Jupp Road. It would look pretty crude these days but then it was quite the place to go, with the height of modern amenities. It didn't have changing rooms as such, but instead had rows of cubicles around the edge of the pool. When a session ended the pool used to be emptied; nothing sophisticated, they just pulled a plug out of the bottom. For the boys this was a challenge, and they used to dive into the ever-decreasing water. To make it really hair-raising they would dive off the top of the cubicles. Well, this time they were doing the performance as usual but just as Fred dived somebody threw a pair of swimming trunks at him. They hit him in the face, and I suppose they blinded him for an instant.

Anyway, it completely messed up his judgement and he landed square on his head on the bottom of the pool.

He was in quite a state with blood everywhere, but he climbed out of the pool and looked at his head in the mirror. As he parted his hair to look at the wound he realised that he could actually see his skull, the skin had completely burst apart. You did not have to be a genius to know that he would have to go to hospital to get it stitched up. So he got changed and trooped off to the hospital with his mates – and remember that there were no ambulances in those days – so he walked from Jupp Road all the way to Queen Mary's in West Ham Lane, which must have been at least a mile or so. When he got there they stitched him up, but said that he should stay in overnight for observation. It was all a bit of an adventure so he stayed. Next morning the nurses were still not happy so they called for the doctor to look at him again. The doctor prescribed some medicine or other and they prepared to give it to him.

'Open your mouth,' said the nurse.

'It is open,' replied Fred.

'Well open it wide,' she said.

'It is open wide,' insisted Fred.

And that was the first they discovered that there was something drastically wrong between what he could feel and what he could control! The doctor came back again and this time, after very careful examination, discovered that he had completely split one of the vertebrae at the top of his spine from top to bottom. They didn't have all those collars and pulleys and things in those days so they laid him flat on his back and packed all round his head, neck and shoulders with sandbags to keep him totally still. And that was how he stayed for weeks.

Of course, when I heard the story from Frankie I was really horrified and felt terribly sorry for the poor bloke. So sorry, in fact, that I asked if I could go and visit him even though I barely knew him. Not possible, Frankie explained. Because he must not move at all he wasn't allowed any visitors.

'Not even his mother?' I asked.

'He hasn't got a mother,' Frankie replied, and then I heard the story of Fred's life. It was the sort of story you barely like to think about now but it was all too common in those days. His mother had been the dresser to Kate Carney, who was one of the big music hall stars up in London. His father was taken on as her coachman and I suppose the pair of them spent a lot of time waiting around at theatres and the like so they soon got together and got married. Soon after Fred was born his father died [Editor's note: according to the Birth Certificate his father died before he was born] but his mother didn't stay single for long and she remarried. All Fred's brothers and sisters were by this second marriage and they all took their dad's name but Fred kept his. Then his mother died! Can you imagine how the poor kid must have felt. Still, all credit to Charlie Paternoster, he brought all those kids up as his own without any favouritism or difference between them. It must have been really hard though, and they suffered the sort of poverty that even I never knew. I can say that because they lived in the part of Stratford that even we looked down on, and never went to because it was so 'bad'. I suppose it was the circumstances but your dad was always a bit apart from the rest of the family and used to do his own thing a lot of the time. Fair's fair, though, he always looked after the old man as if he was his own father and in his old age used to visit every week and keep him in tobacco. When the old boy died his real children insisted that Fred was 'the eldest son' and should lead the mourners. I think Fred was quite taken aback, but he very much appreciated the gesture. Anyway I, of course, only heard the story as far as his mother dying but that was enough to make me sorry beyond words for the poor fellow and decided I would have to get to know him when he came out of hospital.

Eventually he did come out of hospital. Then the boys were all into motorbikes, which was something else my mother warned me about. The very next day after he came out of hospital he went down to Eastbourne on somebody's pillion. You would have thought he would have been more careful. Talking of which, one of the boys was my friend Lucy's brother and he got engaged to a girl named Chrissie from the other side of Stratford. He was killed in a motorbike accident but Lucy, Chrissie and I remained friends ever since [Editor's note: in fact until they died], though Chrissie never took up with anybody else and stayed single. I think that Fred got well known in the hospital and he certainly appreciated all they did for him because he went onto their blood-donors panel. Those were the early days of blood transfusion when you laid side-by-side with the person you were donating to, and got a certificate to tell you the outcome. I've still got one of them somewhere. Anyway, I made the effort to meet Fred, talk to him, and eventually we got together. That quite upset my mother, especially because of his accident. She firmly believed it must have caused some weakness and always maintained 'that he wouldn't make old bones' so you can guess how she reacted when I told her we were going to get married!

Anyway, we got married on 20 February 1932. It was a bit of a shock when we woke up to find thick snow on the ground, but it did not deter Mum from

TELEPHONE SYDENHAM 3040

British · Red · Cross · Society.

BLOOD TRANSFUSION SERVICE.

TELEPHONE:
New Cross 1606.

1928/1018

5, COLYTON ROAD, S.E. 22.

3/11/28.   Mr. F.F. Smith.

The Hon. Secretary has pleasure in forwarding copy of the official report of the Surgeon in reference to the case of blood transfusion recently served by you.

Date of Transfusion   21st. October, 1928

Hospital   Guy's

Ward   Miriam   Doctor   G.W. Rake

Name of Donor   Mr. F.F. Smith

Sex of Patient   Female   Age   25   Group   IV

Nature of Disease or Injury

Spleno medullary Leukaemia

Approximate amount of blood taken   400   cc.
(426 c.c. equals $\frac{3}{4}$ pint.)
Result of Transfusion, so far as can be ascertained

Slight immediate improvement in patient's condition, which has since been maintained.

P. L. OLIVER, Hon. Secretary.

Certificate of direct donor-to-patient blood donation.

any of her plans. Nobody could afford to hire halls or anything like that for the reception, and so we got married from home. The first job, then, was to make room for the party and, never mind the snow, we carried most of the furniture out into the backyard. In fact, pretty well everything except Mum's bed – her bed wasn't going to stand out in the snow! We also needed somewhere to hang the coats, but that too was easily solved. Mum bought a couple of ounces of 6in nails and simply drove them into the wall of the small bedroom.

We got married in St John's Church, Stratford. Fred was ever so well known around Stratford, and as we drove back from the church all the stall-holders and quite a few of the passers-by stopped to cheer, shout their best wishes, and all the rest. It really was quite some fun. Back home, Mum had laid on a full hot meal wedding breakfast. She bought and cooked two aitch-bones of beef and two hams all in our tiny little kitchen, while Dad had used his market job to get loads of potatoes and fresh salad, including cucumbers and tomatoes. That might seem pretty ordinary now, but back in 1932 fresh salad in February was almost unheard of.

The big disadvantage of having the reception at home was that it was too small for everybody to sit down together so we ate in two sittings! Dad, as ever, hadn't come straight back home from the church and instead stopped at the pub on the way. Just as the first sitting was finishing its meal he arrived back, already well drunk and in high spirits. He was also terribly pleased with himself.

''Ere Doll!' he shouted up the stairs as he came in, 'look who I ran into on my way home. We stopped for a drink at the pub and I bought them home for a meal.' 'They' were Fred's mum and dad (well, his step-mum and dad) so where on earth did he think they were going before he waylaid them into the pub? The party went on well into the night and spread all over the house, up and down the stairs, and out into the road. Just across the road from our house was a cast-iron public urinal and my lasting memory of that day was seeing everybody linking hands around this urinal to play ring-a-ring-a-roses.

15

The Second World War

(1939–45)

I suppose it sounds like a joke, but I actually do remember the day that war broke out. Every Sunday we used to go over to the City of London cemetery at Manor Park to visit Dad's grave and then go on to Mum's for the afternoon. Of course, on this particular Sunday there was all sorts of tension in the air and we wanted to wait for the Prime Minister's broadcast at eleven o'clock on the radio. Sure enough, the broadcast came and it was war. Suddenly, all the old routines went out the window. We decided to go over and see sister Doll instead. By now she had two children and had been told that if there was war she would be evacuated. We wanted to see her before she went. It sounds silly now; as if anything would have got sorted out on the first afternoon of the war. Still, we were young and naïve, and at first you thought that the government knew what it was doing. We learned pretty quickly, but these were early days. So we walked round to Doll's, but she wasn't there. It turns out that, because of the children, she had been told to report to the school around the corner to arrange for evacuation.

As we were walking back home the air raid alarm went off. Of course, it was a false alarm but we didn't know that at the time. You wouldn't believe the panic and confusion, because nobody had the faintest idea what to do. Then somebody said it was a gas attack. This was always the great fear at the start of the war; I suppose it was a hangover from the stories of the First World War.

We had already been issued with gas masks so lots of people put them on. I can still remember walking up the street with people standing at their doorways wearing gas masks and looking up at the sky searching for the bombers.

Anyway, Doll told us later that she had gone round to the school and was waiting in the playground when the warning went off. They were all hustled inside 'for protection', I think that later on that would have been seen as a mistake – if you couldn't get into a proper shelter it was better to stay out in the open. Just as she reached the door of the school the excitement, the heat, and no doubt the worry of the two kids, finally got the better of Doll and she fainted. Apparently, a man rushed off to get her a drink of water but had no idea where the kitchens or anything were and so, in desperation, grabbed a vase of flowers, threw out the flowers and gave Doll the water! She still remembers waking up with little leaves stuck all around her mouth.

In fact, Doll soon got a house out in Buckhurst Hill so she was out of the real danger. Her husband was called up into the army straight away at the start of the war and was soon away in France. One day Doll was cleaning her windows when she saw this soldier coming up the street. He was in a dreadful state; a total wreck, scruffy and staggering all over the place. He looked more like a tramp than a soldier. She assumed he must be totally drunk and was quite scandalised, but she watched him steadily making his way towards her. Eventually he stopped at the little wall in front of the house and looked up at Doll, who was still standing at the window watching him.

'Let me in, Doll,' he said.

It was her husband just back from Dunkirk. The effect of the exhaustion, the strain, the battering and all the rest had changed him so much that she hadn't recognised him. He had got back with nothing except the clothes he was wearing – he had even lost his tin hat. It must have been bad, because my brother Bob always maintained that the one thing you never took off, never let go of, hung on to at all costs, was your tin hat. Your rifle might get 'too heavy' or 'get in the way', but you wore your tin hat to the last.

Those early days were pretty chaotic and Hitler could have had anything he wanted if he had bothered to turn up. Fred's brother George was working down on the south coast, where he joined the Home Guard. He was given a large spike and told to protect the coast from invasion! Nobody told him what to do with this spike if the invasion did come, but he still swears that he saw it approaching at least half-a-dozen times on his first night of sentry duty. My sister's husband-to-be, also a George, was also in the Home Guard. They had an anti-invasion exercise one night and he was ever so excited because

Fred and Polly at about the time of their wedding (1932).

his platoon had been chosen as one of the attackers. With all the anti-German feeling around we couldn't understand why anybody would even want to play-act being a German. But, he explained, the defenders were on duty all night while the attackers were sooner or later rounded up and then sent back to the HQ where they could have a cup of cocoa. It was much better to be an attacker.

The war took quite a toll, though. Fred was in a reserved occupation – he was a toolmaker – though he was silly enough to volunteer. When he told the recruiting officer what job he did he got sent home with a flea in his ear for wasting their time! Apart from him, though, all my brothers, and most of the other men I knew, ended up in the forces. None of them was killed, in fact none was physically wounded, but looking back most of them paid a high price for their service. Daisy's husband John was blown up in the desert. He was in the artillery and his gun got a direct hit. I suppose it must have set off some of the ammunition because there was an enormous explosion and all that was left was a hole in the ground. Anyway, John was assumed dead, along with all the other blokes who were never found, but a couple of days later he wandered in from the desert. He didn't know who he was, what he had done, or where he had been. He was eventually invalided home but was always a bit vacant, and had to be told what to do next. If they were going out he had to be told to put his shoes on because otherwise he would carry on wearing his slippers. He became a bit of a joke among people who had not known him before the war. But honestly, when he went off into the army he was the finest man who ever walked God's earth; the man who came back was nothing like the man who went out. It was heartbreaking.

Looking back, most of my friends and relatives who were in the forces seemed to end up in the desert and then Italy. Eddy, my friend's husband, was captured in the desert and spent the rest of the war as a PoW. On his first day home after the war he sat at the kitchen table, looked at the wall opposite, and said that if there was another war he would go again, he would fight if he had to, but he would never be taken prisoner again. He never said another word about his experiences. My brother-in-law Bert never said anything either, not until almost his last words that is. In the late 1980s he spent his last days in a local hospice and by the end wasn't really conscious. As far as we could tell, he didn't know what was going on around him and barely spoke. However, one day a priest went in to see him. Bert didn't look at him or even open his eyes, but must have sensed the priest and was quite rude.

'You can go away,' he said, 'I'll never get to heaven. I killed a man in the war and I never even knew his name.' He had never said anything about any such incident, and we have no idea what happened, but it must have been preying on his mind all those years. He had never got over it.

My brother Bob went all through the desert and then on into Italy. In fact, every year at Christmas I still have to weep when the news on TV reports that the Pope has given his blessing to the 'City and the World' – and especially when television shows the picture of the crowds in St Peter's Square. You see, I listened to the live radio broadcast from Rome on Christmas Day 1944. I cannot remember who the reporter was or anything like that, but he was talking about the vast crowd of mainly servicemen crowding the square with their eyes glued to the balcony of the Vatican (or wherever it was that the Pope appears). Then he turned his attention to 'a lone RASC driver, sitting on the running board of his lorry parked just beyond the edge of the crowd and enjoying a cigarette.' After the war Bob told us how on Christmas Day there really wasn't very much to do so he volunteered to drive the Catholics from his unit into Rome to see the Pope, and how he watched it all sitting on the running board of his lorry. So that must have been him. It sent a shiver up my spine then, and it still does every year.

I said that I remembered the day the war broke out. I also remember the day the war ended, or at least, the day it ended in Europe – VE Day. We had, by then, been bombed out of Keogh Road and they moved us into a half-house about half a mile away in Earlham Grove. We had the ground floor and another family lived upstairs. Anyway, on VE Day I was at home on my own, apart from the kids that is. Somehow you felt that you had to do something, but there was nothing to do. I couldn't think of anything better than to stand at the front gate and find somebody to talk to. Even then, the street was pretty well empty. It was very long and right up at the far end I could see a young woman coming along. I stood there and watched her, thinking of all the wonderful things I could say and how happy we would be. Eventually she got within speaking range.

'It's over at last then,' said I, all bright and breezy.

'Sorry,' she said, 'I can't celebrate. My brother is a prisoner of war with the Japs. I can't celebrate.'

And she went on her way. She had such hatred in her eyes and voice, I really couldn't credit it. It knocked me back on my heels and knocked me down for the rest of the day. I never saw her again and I've got no idea what happened to her brother, even whether he ever came back. The way the Japs treated prisoners was unbelievable and nothing is enough to pay them back for their behaviour. I have often felt I would like to meet the man who dropped the atom bomb on them and shake him by the hand. That must have been the best thing that was done in the whole war. Even that was a better death than they gave to PoWs.

16

The Blitz

(1940–4)

I get really sick of all the rubbish about the Blitz and the cheerful East Enders who refused to be downhearted. It wasn't like that at all. It was bloody awful and the authorities were just not prepared. As always, it was the ordinary people who just had to put up with the suffering and grief caused by the mistakes and stupidity of those who claimed to know best. Poor bloody devils.

I remember the first day of the Blitz. We were living in Keogh Road then, and I was expecting the first boy so I was a great lump. Fred was at work. You worked every hour God sent then; you just went into work and stayed; you didn't have any option. My friend Chrissie came round to see me and said that if we went up the Point [Editor's note: Maryland Point] to the wool shop she would buy some silk and crochet a dress for the baby. It sounded a good idea so I started to get ready.

Just then, Fred walked in. He looked awful. He told us that he had just had enough – I cannot remember how long he had been at work by then – and he couldn't carry on any longer, so he had come home. I got in a bit of a flap because I hadn't got any dinner ready, in fact I hadn't even thought about it yet and was only just getting ready to go shopping. What could I do for him? What did he want? and all that. But he didn't care, he couldn't care less, he just wanted to rest and told me not to bother but go shopping. He went into the front room (we were ever so posh because we had a front room with some decent furniture) sat in an armchair and almost instantly went to sleep. I finished getting ready and, with Chrissie, went up the shops. When we got back Fred was still in the chair asleep. I don't think he had moved a muscle while we were out. He must have been absolutely knackered.

I was about to start preparing some food when the warning went. Chrissie flew into a panic about getting down the shelter. We didn't have our own shelter but Aunty next door had an Anderson shelter and we shared that. We had even knocked down a section of the wall between the gardens so that we could go in and out easily. It had been quite useful really because Uncle had been having some medical trouble and I had been able to nip in and help when he had one of his 'attacks'. I had even been up to the hospital with him a couple of times. Anyway, Chrissie was flapping up and down about the warning and the shelter, but of course she worked out of London all week and only came back at weekends so she didn't understand how we had got used to it during the Battle of Britain. The warning was always going but nothing ever happened because the Germans were attacking the airfields, not London. After a while we had stopped taking notice of them and got on with our lives as if nothing had happened, just like I wanted to start getting the dinner ready. But she went on and on, so in the end I said that I would go down the shelter. First, though, I had to wake Fred, which wasn't very easy. When I eventually managed and told him what was going on he started on me too – I should have gone straight to the shelter, it didn't matter about the false alarms, there was no time to hang about, and all the rest. Anybody would have thought that the warning was all my fault!

So nursing my lump I picked my way over the rubble of the wall. Chrissie was already down in the shelter, she had shot out there as soon as I had said the word, and Fred was behind me fussing. I got to the door and was just about to take the first step down when there was an almighty thump and I found myself laying flat on the lump in the middle of the floor. A bomb had landed about 50 yards away! Luckily it hadn't exploded, but just the force of hitting the ground had made the thump and there was a crater in the road. Boy did we jump into that shelter. There was only a dirt floor and nothing to sit on. I mean, up until then we had not taken it very seriously so there were no preparations or efforts to make it comfortable.

We weren't there long, because once they realised about the unexploded bomb we all had to move out. They tried to move us down to the local school which had been opened to provide emergency accommodation, but I did not fancy that. Instead Fred took me down to my mum's which was on the other side of Stratford.

We hadn't been there long either when my brother came in from work. He worked in the same place as Fred, down in the docks area, but because of the bombing they had been sent home. He was an amazing sight, ever so scruffy and untidy, but BLACK! Because of the bombing there were no buses so he had to walk home. But that meant walking all the way through the docks which had been the main target. Wherever he went there were fires and wreckage, and many of the roads had been closed but the firemen let him through because he was trying to get home. By the time he had walked in, through and past all these fires, he was totally black.

He was going out with a girl in Canning Town at the time, and of course that had got more of a pasting than us even. As soon as he got cleaned up he wanted to go out again to see if she was alright. Mum started kicking up a fuss about the danger and how he should stay at home. In the end Fred came up with the solution – he put a saucepan lid inside my brother's cap to protect him! It did not fit in very easily and goodness knows how he kept it on his head. I do not think I had laughed so much for years but it made Mum happier so he left.

Then the warning went again. We did not mess about this time but headed straight for the shelter. To be honest, Mum's shelter wasn't worth the bother. It was only set a few inches into the soil and there was barely any soil on top of it, just about enough to grow some lettuces later in the war if I remember rightly. Still, we got into it, or would have done if it had been big enough. Just like Aunty's back in Keogh Road it had no furniture or other comforts, though they would have made it more cramped. Fred stood just outside and whenever he heard a bomb coming close he would squeeze inside the door.

We spent the night like that. It was the most terrible night. Next morning we went back home but they still wouldn't let us in because the bomb hadn't been dealt with. I cannot remember what we did but we must have got back sometime that day. That was the first day of the Blitz.

It was all a pretty terrifying experience and I must admit that after a little while I thought that we had really had enough. I just couldn't see how we could possibly carry on having hell knocked out of us every night and I was all in favour of Mr Churchill asking for peace on whatever terms were available. I even said as much to Fred, but he didn't reply. Then one day I went up to London with him. The Swimming Club had all sorts of silver cups and trophies and it had been decided that these should be put into safe custody in some big bank up in the City. There had been a raid the night before and as we travelled I remember looking at some of the grand buildings all battered and smashed, and suddenly I got angry. In that moment my mood turned round completely, and I still remember thinking that we weren't going to let that 'bloody barbarian' destroy everything. We would stop him and punish him, whatever it took.

My sister-in-law Doll was in her shelter on the night when the sewer-bank [Editor's note: the Northern Outfall Sewer which runs through an artificial embankment to the Beckton Sewage Works] was hit. All the lights went out as well, which added to the confusion. Suddenly water started flowing into the shelter and it quickly reached a few feet deep. It was time to get out and Dolly started to feel her way to the door. Her hand came against something floating so she carefully picked it up and held it until she got outside. Then, in the better light she looked down and saw she was carrying a turd. She rushed indoors to wash her hands but found the lower floor also flooded. The water drained away fairly quickly but, when she opened the knife drawer in her kitchen cabinet, she found another turd nestled nicely among the cutlery.

In the end she was bombed out of the East End but managed to get half a house in Roding Valley, away from the real bombing. Doll was really pleased to find somewhere that was so much safer than London and always wanted me to stay with her or at the very least, whenever I visited, to delay my return from there until the last possible moment. I used to visit her at least once a week. It was quite a performance, especially with the baby. I used to have to walk through to the Point and get a bus up to Leytonstone High Road. There I would get the train out to Buckhurst Hill and walk from there to Doll's. The return journey was simply the reverse.

One day there were all sorts of hold-ups along the Leytonstone Road, hangovers from the bombing I suppose, and when I reached the station the train was already in. I could see it at the other side of the platform, but from the bus stop I had to walk all round the outside of the station to come in from the other side. I shot off as fast as I could and halfway round met a railwayman. I was pretty desperate so I asked him if there was any way he could hold up the train while I got round the outside.

'Don't bother,' he said, 'follow me,' and he led me through a little tunnel straight up onto the platform. It struck me right away what a useful short cut it was, and how it was a pretty good shelter in an emergency. Anyway, I caught the train.

As the afternoon wore on I decided to leave early. Doll was ever so upset and wanted me to stay longer. Fred always encouraged me to stay as well, he always thought it was too dangerous for me to go back into town. But, somehow, I felt I had to get Robert into bed early and I was determined to get him to bed. So I left a bit earlier than usual, getting home earlier, and putting him to bed earlier.

The next week I set off as usual to visit Doll. Having found the short cut there seemed no reason to go the long way round the station. Only, when I got there, the entrance passageway to the tunnel was blocked by a barrier. So, once again I walked around the outside. Still, I had plenty of time, and when I eventually reached the platform I asked the porter why the tunnel was closed.

'Bad business' he said. Apparently the week before the warning had gone just as my 'later' train reached the platform. For protection, all the passengers had been ushered down into the tunnel. That is where they were when it received a direct hit and everybody was killed. Of course, it was wartime, and we had heard nothing about it in the news or local papers. It was just coincidence that I met somebody able to tell me the story.

After the Blitz it all went rather quiet, the raids more or less stopped and life sort of got back to normal. That was, until the doodlebugs towards the end of the war. I can remember the first couple ever so clearly. The first was completely unexpected – the warning went but it had been ages since there was any sort of raid and nothing seemed to be going on in the sky so we didn't take it seriously. Suddenly there was a loud bang, obviously a long way away, but obviously very big. That one fell on Upton Park, but of course no official explanation was given. The next day there was another warning. Fred was around for some reason and doing his air raid warden routine. He kept saying it was alright, this was an exercise because 'they' were worried that air raid drill was getting slack. It was only an exercise so it was important for everybody to go through the routine for practise. The more he said it was an exercise and very important the less interested everybody else got. Then somebody called us out into the street. We ran out and looked up, and there was a small aeroplane flying over 'on fire'! We watched horrified as it went out of sight and a few seconds later came that same bang we had heard the day before. That was the first doodlebug we saw. It fell on Bow and killed a woman and her five children.

After that we started following air-raid drills again.

17

The Dirtiest Woman in the World

(1940–50)

For most of the war we lived in Keogh Road and there was a young woman who lived next door. Her husband was away in the army so we had never seen him from the time we moved in. She had three children, twin girls and a boy. The two girls were real beauties, long blonde hair, clear blue eyes, smooth unblemished skin, and always smiling, always pleasant. But she was ugly, she was unbelievably ugly, the sort of face that made you instinctively either stare in grim fascination or look away in embarrassment and disgust. Then at last her husband got some leave and was coming home for a week. I couldn't wait to see who would or could have married such an impossibly ugly woman. When he finally arrived I got the shock of my life – he truly was one of the most handsome men I have ever seen. Goodness knows how they got together or what he saw in her, but they made the most unlikely couple you could imagine.

Still, no one can help being ugly. But much worse, to my mind, was that she was dirty. Her hands and face were dirty, her hair hung down matted into lank, greasy, cord-like strands, her clothes were dirty, her children were dirty and her house was dirty. The girls were evacuated away from London for a long time but wanted to get back to their mum and were eventually reunited. They turned up clean, beautiful and cared for, with long, flowing blonde hair. Within a couple of days their heads were covered with the same straggling mess of greasy rats' tails as their mother. When her husband came home on that leave they went to bed and in the middle of the night he woke up to find himself covered with fleas. She was literally flea-infested. So he got her up in the middle of his first night of leave and washed her hair in paraffin. Some romantic homecoming. The truth was, she just had absolutely no idea how to look after herself – I suppose that for some reason nobody had ever taught her how. I never knew anything about her childhood or why she should have missed out on such basic upbringing.

She shared the house with an older couple. During the war if you were bombed out you were pleased to get a roof over your head, you didn't think there was anything odd about sharing that roof with whoever the council said you would. The older woman tried her best to help, and really kept them going a lot of the time. From our house I could look through into her kitchen and was absolutely staggered one day to see the family eating their dinner. The older woman had cooked the dinner for them and delivered it in its cooking pots. And there at the table were the four of them eating, one from a plate, one from a pudding basin, one from the potato saucepan and one from its lid! Can you imagine eating your dinner from the saucepan lid?

Those houses had a 2ft-wide 'front' surrounded by a low wall against the pavement. One day I went out and she was sitting on her front wall crying.

'My little Tommy's got chicken pox; why has my little Tommy got chicken pox?' she wailed. And she alternated floods of tears with the same despairing cry. The poor little devil was lucky just to have chicken pox when you think of the squalor he lived in. Anyway, of course the pox sores got infected and started to ooze pus and muck so that he had to go to hospital. I can still remember seeing him going out of the house. Apparently they slept in beds directly on the mattress and covered by blankets, no sign of a sheet. I don't know whether she couldn't afford sheets or whether she just had no idea about how to use them. Anyway, the poor little kid had been laying in bed suffering from his chicken pox and the infected sores on top of that. As the sores had oozed the blankets had stuck to the pus and blood so that he was just stuck to his bedclothes. When the ambulance men came they had to cut out the bits of blanket round the sores. And that is how he came out of the house, laying on a stretcher with circular patches of blanket stuck to his sores. He must have been tough though, because he recovered.

We lost touch with them when we were bombed out. That was by a doodlebug in late 1944 though their house next door was almost untouched! I moved in with my sister for a short while, while Fred slept at his ARP post. Eventually we got the half-house in Earlham Grove so didn't see much more of them. For all I could say, there must have been love in that family because they stuck together and looked after each other. After the war the mother became very ill. I used to see her out shopping with the two girls. One of them was married by then and had a baby in a pram. Sometimes the mother would support herself on the pram and sometimes the girls would take an arm each to support her. She died soon after. I often wondered what happened to her little Tommy, and her very handsome husband.

18

War Babies

(1940–5)

My eldest boy was born in 1940, right in the middle of the London Blitz. I wanted to have the baby at home and that was the plan, right up until pretty well the last moment. In those days they said you had to stay in bed after a baby was born so you had to have somebody to look after you. Well, I asked around and a woman round the corner said she would come in every day. Between her and my mum the hospital decided that I had enough people to look after me so it was all OK. Then, at a routine hospital visit they asked me some question or other about this woman round the corner and when I went to see her about it there was no house and no woman. They had just disappeared in a raid. Well that put the cap on that plan! Of course, with all the raids going on it wasn't possible for me to go into the hospital there. The only possibility was to be evacuated somewhere and so they gave me a note and sent me round to the Evacuation Office in the town hall the next morning.

So off I went to the town hall. There had been a raid the night before and, although the town hall hadn't been hit, it had been pretty badly shaken by the bombing and the whole building was really a bit of a shambles. What was worse, the Evacuation Office was right up on the top floor and the girl on the counter at the entrance just pointed me up some stairs which rose from the back of the entrance hall. These stairs were thick with rubble and everything

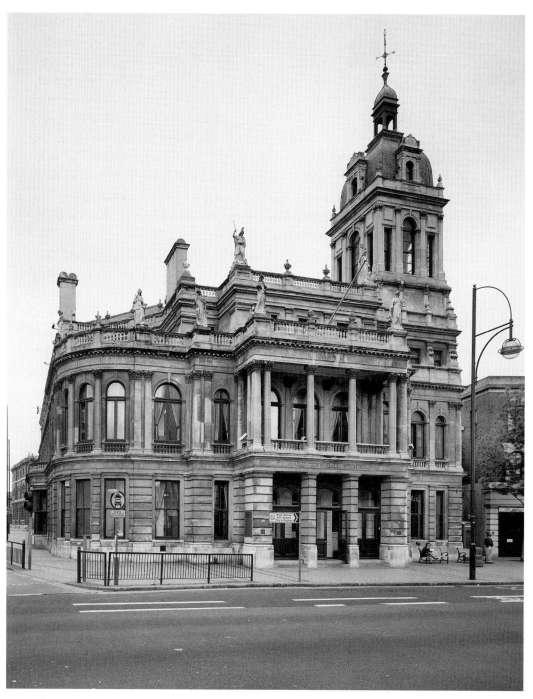

Stratford Town Hall, home of the area's Evacuation Office.
© Crown Copright, National Monument Record.

was covered with plaster dust that had shaken down from the ceiling. Looking back on it, I'm not sure that they were safe for anybody to go up, let alone me with an almighty great lump. But then again, at the time everybody had their problems and you couldn't make special arrangements just because somebody was going to have a baby. To be honest, you didn't even bother to think that special arrangements might be a good idea; you just got on with life whatever you had to do. Eventually I picked my way over the rubble, got to the top of the stairs and found the office. They asked all sorts of questions, took down all sorts of details, filled in this and that, gave me a card and told me to report at the baby clinic next morning. The clinic was also the departure point for evacuation.

Fred managed to take a half-day off and was going to take me up to the clinic so that he could find out where I was going. That night there was yet another raid and when we arrived at the Broadway the whole place was closed off. The woodyard was on fire, piles of rubble lay across the road, fire hoses snaked across all over the place and firemen were still running around trying to put out the fires from the night before. The whole area was surrounded by a barrier and a couple of policemen were watching it to stop anybody getting too close. Well, that was no help to me so I called the policeman over and told him I had to get across to the clinic because I was supposed to be evacuated to have the baby. At first he said that it was impossible but eventually it was agreed that a fireman could escort me through the danger zone to the clinic. But only me; he couldn't spare the effort to look after Fred. And that was that. We just said goodbye there and then and off I went – nothing else to be done. He had no idea what I was doing, where I was going, whether he would ever see me again. I know that having a baby isn't easy anytime, but at least I knew what was going on. I honestly wonder how the men coped. It must have been terrible just seeing your wife go off, goodness knows where, with no time to say anything.

We got on a coach which took us all over the place but nowhere could take us in until, at last, we arrived in rural Hertfordshire, at a large house in Ware that had just been taken over as a sort of maternity unit. It was the home of Lord and Lady somebody, but he had died and she had just gone off and married the vicar. She moved down to the vicarage and let the government have the house 'for the duration'. We were very lucky really because just at the same time as we arrived a party of nurses from the London [Hospital] arrived to run the place. They were absolutely marvellous.

There was no proper hospital furniture. A load of hospital beds had been sent down with some blankets, but nothing more – no sheets, or pillowcases or anything. Anyway, these beds were put up in some of the big rooms and that was that. Before we went to bed we wanted something to eat. Well, we hadn't eaten all day. So we told the nurses and they looked a bit lost. After a couple of minutes though they said we should follow them. So we did, down to the kitchens. There they gave us bread and cheese. Just that, bread and cheese, no butter or anything to go with it. Well, there was a cup of weak tea. We were not very happy but it had to do, and so we went to bed. That night we just had the blankets and we had to put our coats on the bottom of the bed in case there was a raid. Next morning when we got up I was livid. I had just bought a new dark blue overcoat and I was ever so pleased with it – thought I looked the real cat's whiskers. Next morning it was covered with white fluff from the blanket! It took me ages to tidy it up again. A little while later we realised that we had eaten the nurses' food; it was what they had brought down from London with them for their own supper and they just went hungry. I told you that they were marvellous.

They really were wonderful people and they did an amazing job. The next day the food began to arrive so we had something to eat from then on. Mind you, the food was awful because they had no idea how to cook. I suppose none of them had ever had to cook before and certainly not for a maternity hospital full of women. One day they asked what we wanted and somebody said neck of lamb stew. One of them went off to the butcher's with our ration books – we had to give in our books when we arrived – and came back with best-end chops. Well, that's not the point of stew; what you want is the cheap scrag-end and get a lot more of it for your money. Anyway, they stewed the meat and come lunchtime there we were with our mouths watering. When the food came up you would never believe what they had done – on each plate was a couple of potatoes and a small piece of this meat. They had only drained off the liquid to use as soup for our supper. One of the girls was ever so upset, asked why she couldn't have her ration book back and go back to London. She was sure she could manage better than the nurses!

One day they asked if we could help with some housework. About time really, because these poor girls couldn't hope to do all the work that had to be done. They were only the usual nursing staff for a hospital, but they were meant to be doing the housekeeping, keeping this house running and everything else as well. Most of us volunteered, so they gave us dusters and mops and things and off we went. Downstairs, along a passage, and then into the servants' quarters was where the nurses were living. Talk about having your eyes opened! It was real squalor; they had absolutely nothing down there. No carpets on the floor, no chairs, nothing. I went to do staff-nurse-whatever's room and I was shocked. I mean, we were from the East End and had seen most things but this was dreadful. She had a double bed spring base with a single mattress pushed against the wall so that when she went to bed she had to crawl across the springs. On the bed she had a single blanket, no sheets or anything. I was so shocked I called all the others in to see how she was living. I don't think we complained very much after that.

We had a couple of warnings, not raids, because who was going to bomb a country village? We honestly didn't bother very much because we knew that they were only flying over to bomb some other poor sod in London. And anyway, by then we had all got pretty used to it in London. The nurses, though, had to get us up and into the shelter. Mind you, it wasn't much of a shelter. They cleared out the space under the stairs, even if it was an enormous staircase, and put some chairs in it. The first night that there was a warning was absolute bedlam. They got us all down in the shelter, but there wasn't enough room. The nurses all stood around outside in the hall. One woman was in the middle of labour and she was hanging on the stair rails moaning, yelling, and saying 'never-a-bloody-gain' (or words to that effect). She wasn't getting much sympathy from the rest of us though and there was a constant running commentary going both ways. Later, one of the nurses told me she had been to all the London shows but had never had such an hilarious night as that one. I suppose we had to calm our own nerves and we knew the bombs were not for us.

Mind you, the locals weren't too sure about it all. One night a couple of bombs were dropped just outside the village. It must have been some sort of accident, the pilot got lost or was shot up or something, because nobody could have deliberately bothered to bomb such a nowhere place. Next day I was proudly pushing my new baby through the village in the pram with one of the other girls when, a few yards ahead, a door suddenly opened and this old woman stepped out on the pavement with a face like thunder. She shook her fist at us, and until then I didn't realise that people shook their fists in real life and not just in books. She shouted out that it was all our fault – 'Hitler's bloody followed you!' she screamed. Goodness knows why she thought Hitler would order his bombers to follow two young pregnant women out of the East End of London so as to bomb them in the country as well.

My younger boy was born at the other end of the war when the only remaining hazard was the rockets. By then I had been evacuated to rural Cambridgeshire, but when I looked at the local hospitals I decided I would rather risk the rockets. Somehow they seemed a lot less dangerous than a country hospital. Fred wasn't very keen on the idea and tried to persuade me not to come back. He wrote a letter over three days listing all the incidents as they happened and what the results were [Editor's note: the complete text can be found at the end of this chapter]. I still thought that it was safer than a country hospital and so I returned to London when the baby was nearly due. Our house had been destroyed a few months before by a doodlebug and we were living in the downstairs half of a requisitioned house a couple of streets away.

Well, this day I suddenly started into labour. So I had a quick bath and then called Mrs J – she was the lady who had the other half of the house – and she came with me off to the hospital. We had just got off the bus in the Broadway when I got the most almighty whopper of a pain and I was doubled up with it in the doorway of the cinema when the warning went! Well, we couldn't help that, and once the pain had passed we walked the last couple of hundred yards to the hospital.

Now, whenever an alarm sounded the hospital went onto standby, so by the time we arrived all the doors were closed and there was no way in. Anyway, we went up to the door and rang the bell. After a couple of moments an irate nurse appeared and before either of us could speak began to read the riot act to us. There was a war on, didn't we hear the warning?, no visitors could possibly come in, what about possible casualties, at which she paused for breath and I managed to get in that I was 'not a visitor but a customer'. That quite caught her fancy and for the whole of my stay I was called 'the customer'. Anyway, her arm shot out, I was pulled in, and the door slammed shut leaving Mrs J standing outside. There was no time for ceremony.

I was rushed through to maternity, helped into a hospital gown, put on the table but, just as the nurse was about to examine me, there was a tremendous bang. A rocket had landed just a couple of streets away. I was blown up in the air and felt as if I was on my way across the room but the nurse's reflexes were up to the occasion and she just managed to catch me and push me down onto the table again. In moments the alarm bell rang – this meant major causalities coming in and the staff had to drop whatever they were doing to get down to the reception area. So she just told me to hang on and rushed away.

So there I was. After a few moments I realised that the woman in the next cubicle was having a terrible time, or so it sounded. She was moaning and groaning. Every now and again she let out an awful animal noise. But still nobody arrived. My pains were getting much more frequent and I was getting nervous, so I started shouting for help. Eventually a nurse came and started to examine me. I tried to get her to look at the woman next door but she sternly replied that I had to deal with my own problems, not hers. Within a very short while the baby was born. The nurse cut and tied the cord and, lacking anything else, wrapped the baby in a dirty towel and gave it to me to nurse. Then she rushed out again back to casualty. It must have been at least an hour until anybody reappeared. I thought I had been forgotten. Obviously the immediate casualty crisis had been dealt with and the staff were a bit calmer now. They started cleaning me up, and suddenly realised that there was no afterbirth! Another panic, but eventually the midwife managed to massage it out.

All that remained was to get me up onto the ward. Fortunately a bed had 'just become vacant', only when they got me up there the bed was still in the same state as the last occupant had left it and they realised they had no clean sheets. After a hurried consultation they decided to use the dirty sheet on which I had just delivered the baby, saying that 'it was, after all, her own dirt.' So in a couple of moments there I was, sat in bed waiting for the nurse to bring my new baby. Suddenly a woman, another patient, arrived at the end of my bed, looked at me in horror as her mouth dropped open – 'Blimey' she said, 'I know that they are short of beds but I only went out for a wash!' She was due to leave that day but the nurses had got a bit ahead of themselves.

When that was eventually sorted out the nurse appeared carrying my new baby, tightly wrapped in a piece of blanket. As soon as the nurse had gone I unwrapped him to have another look. I had never seen anything like it. He was dressed in two woollen matinee jackets. They had obviously been over-washed, over and over again. They were matted and stiff like cardboard. One was put on the right way round and tied with tapes at the collar. The second was then put on back to front over the top and tied again. I was pretty annoyed because all the family had been collecting wool oddments and knitting for me, so the baby had a wonderful 'wardrobe' ready and waiting. I had a go at the nurse, and said I would get my own clothes in but she said that was against the rules because they got 'lost'. I suppose they got pinched. I did dress him in his own clothes to go home though. All the nurses wanted to give him a cuddle because he looked so lovely. Well, I had all the clothes left over from the eldest and all the stuff the family had got together. He looked like a real baby going home and I suppose a lot of the nurses hadn't seen one of them for years!

My only thought then was to get back to the safety of rural Cambridgeshire. As soon as I left the hospital I sent a telegram to Aunty Blinco [Editor's note: the lady of the house where Polly was evacuated to escape the V1/V2 campaigns – see also p. 101 and p. 108] and asked if I could go back. By return came a telegram saying, simply, 'COME COME COME COME'. So I came.

* * *

The unchanged text of a letter from Fred reporting incidents over a three-day period in an effort to dissuade his wife from returning to London.

77 Keogh Road
Thursday
Dear Poll,

Have arrived home safely after a rather quick trip getting to Mum's about 5.50 and hearing a terrible tale of the past week, and living in the shelter which seems to be the wisest thing. They have had 5 or 6 warnings up to then, and I arrived in the middle of one. Since then up until midnight there has been 4 more, making a total of 9 or 10 warnings but have lost count for sure. A warning has just gone shortly after midnight and I suppose this is the all night one so I am off round the post.

Friday:- Have arrived home from work about 5.45 and there is a warning on now the 5th today. First one at 7.10 lasted until 8.35 and we had 4 take covers. The second warning went at 8.50 and lasted until 1.10 and we had 8 take covers. The third went at 1.35 and lasted until 2.45 nothing doing. The next went just after 3 and up until leaving we had 3 take covers making 15 all day, not bad really. I didn't notice the time of the all-clear but it was before 6. The fifth warning went at 6.10 and we have just had a fright; one went right over the top in full view of us all lining the railway fence and dived with a terrific crash in full sight of us somewhere around the Thatched House or Harrow Green – may have a more precise position later. Another one followed about 5 minutes later but he has travelled over much further and we haven't heard the crash although it was quite plain going over. Mrs Butcher is leading off about a lifetime to get a bit of home together and then it gets smashed in a second.

Its quite like blitz times to see everyone in the back yards looking at the sky. It is now just 6.50pm and the 5th all-clear is sounding so I will have to resume with the next warning. Until then a little news. I arrived at Mum's and she made me a cup of tea and I gave her the lettuce & onions and started trying to persuade her down to Son's but it seems pretty useless and I have come to the conclusion that the reason is, that the neighbours are waiting for her to turn her back and then they will flock in & rob her of her home. At least that's what her excuses sound like to me. Jane has offered her the fare. Tiny has as well. Bob sent her £4 to do something about it and I gave her Son's offer but it seems that she won't

The first page of Fred's letter.

do anything about it. I am going to ring up Bob & Maud later as I believe it has been hit badly around there. You remember that rather nice looking blonde girl who we saw when we went over there and you spoke about me blushing. I've heard that she is dying and they have sent for her husband from the Navy. Tell Son that Sister Silwood from the surgery has been killed by a direct hit he will probably know her, the tall one who took over from the old matron. Here goes the 6th to-day and its 7.5 so he doesn't lose much time in between. Mum gave me a tomato last night and that together with the cheese and a lettuce I kept, has made me a nice tea just now and I will be able to have a rake round tomorrow afternoon for something else. I hope you will like this letter Poll but as I promised to let you know exactly what happens I am just putting it down and leaving it to you, what you wish to do, although everyone says you would be mad to come home. I am now going to clear the table have a wash and change and go round the post for a while and will continue with anything that happens later. By the way George Tiney has been to see his wife and kiddies off to Torquay to-day and seems rather worried about it. The 6th all-clear is now going and it is 7.25. Here goes the 7th one and it is now 7.55 still time to beat yesterday's total. Have just returned from the post as one has dropped very close and I think the railway works or Temple Mills got it. Saw it go over and dive, engine still running when it hit. The all-clear for this one went at 9.10 but the 8th warning went at 9.40 and have heard a couple more go down a bit further away this time. The 8th all-clear at 10.10.

I rang Bob up and both he & Maud are quite OK although they were badly blasted on Tuesday night. He told me that he had been to Stevenage (Herts) today and they have had 2 of the bombs there. To resume the next alert has gone at 1.45 Saturday morning and things are a little warm, plenty of banging around as they fall. At 3.45AM one sounded loud enough to send me round the post but it is further over. Another one even louder followed, by one that beat the lot at about 4.30AM so I am staying round the post and giving bed the go-by for tonight. It fell by Manor Rd. station and sent a gas main alight but I think it is mainly a factory area and not a lot of houses around by 'Berks'.

Saturday: left home at 6.20 A.M. warning still on and arrived at the firm to be greeted by a 'Take Cover'. For breakfast I had cheese on toast & bread & dripping which was quite tasty. Worked until 11.45 A.M. with 3 more 'take cover's making it 4 in all. Had Spam & Salad with baked jam roll for dinner and then went straight on to Bearmans from Woolwich but Robert's shoes have not yet arrived and I will call again next week. Arrived home about 1.15 to do a bit of washing and continue this letter and in the meantime we have heard 3 more come down somewhere around. The all-clear has sounded at 1.50 P.M. making that warning a 12 hour one. Another warning has just gone at 2.15 P.M. and it seems crazy to me as to why they sound the all-clear. Two more have just come down, Mrs Jones running for the shelter with her dinner in her hand sure looks funny. 3 o.clock Poll another one down. All-clear sounding now at 3.50 P.M. Here we go again 3.25 warning number 3. All-clear Poll 3.50 P.M. nothing doing this time. Sweet music again number 4 sounding at 4.20 P.M. One down somewhere at 4.25. There goes another tearing over-head like a roll of thunder and it seems to have travelled on for some way by the sound of the crash 4.28 P.M. I was changing my shoes to go out and had to nip just then. All-clear for number 4 going at 4.45 and I think I will go down Mum's for a stroll. The milkman seems late. 5th warning 5.10 one crash all-clear at 5.20. Warning again 6th at 5.40. One more and all-clear at 6 P.M. 7th warning 6.25 2 or 3 bangs this time and the all-clear at 7.30. 8th warning 8 P.M., again one bomb somewhere near and the all-clear at 8.30 9th warning 8.55 very short this time all-clear at 9.10. Here goes the 10th warning today 10 P.M. 2 bombs right over and again the all-clear at 10.30. Plenty of time for more to-day. The 11th warning went at 11.30 and they are coming over at about 5-minute intervals. 5 have crashed down fairly loudly before 12 P.M. A short quiet and then another not so terribly far away. Now after that I get a real scare one is coming straight for me as I am patrolling Louise Rd I dive and a terrific crash brings loads of glass out and I charge off to the Electric Light Office which has got a direct hit. Lots of damage and plenty of houses blasted but I am pleased to say that we have only 16 casualities none of them terribly serious as they were nearly all in shelters. Vicarage Lane is looking very knocked about and we have been working with a searchlight to straighten up a bit At 4.30 A.M I have a lay down and sleep until 6.30 when I go home to go to work.

Sunday:- Arrived at work 7.30 to get a take cover for No 1 warning 7.10 until 7.35. No 2 warning 8 A.M. until 8.20 I take cover and something fairly close. No 3 warning went 9.20 and up until the all-clear at 9.45 there were 5 take covers and plenty around. No 4 warning at 10.35 lasted until 1.45P.M. and again 9 take covers. No more warnings from 1.45 until 5.15 and that is going to be enough for this letter as it will make it exactly 3 days since I got back. It may sound bad Poll but I have given you an exact diary no exaggeration & no kidding I am rather tired as you can guess but I am going to get down to it round the post early tonight and believe me I shan't come out unless it is bad. Hope you and Robert are O.K and would like to think the weather has improved but it is lousy here pouring heavens hard. I will be sending a little parcel for Robert in a day or two and have some Mars & chocolate and one or two little toys. By the way Saturday there were 22 take covers Friday 15 and today 16 making a total of 53 since I came back. You must make your own decision Poll about staying or coming home but if it is any guide to you Salway School has opened up to take evacuee names and the Government are again evacuating people from here. Take care of yourself Poll hope Robert is a good boy and believe me when I say I am quite O.K and will be seeing you for the week-end very shortly if convenient to Son & Els. Tell Bill Plum that so far I have heard nothing about round his way and will write if I do. Let me know if you want anything. The milkman is leaving me a pint every day and I am doing O.K for grub Lots of love to you and all as I can hardly keep my eyes open I going to close and will write again very shortly. All the best Poll don't worry about anything as it is not so bad

Love to All
Yours Fred
Xxxxxxx

Robert from Daddy
xxxxxx

19

Farewell to Arms

(1940–3)

My brother Bob was called up very early in the war. In fact he was part of the 'second militia' – though I don't know what that name was supposed to mean and who the 'first militia' were. Anyway, he got his call-up papers and, I think, was quite looking forward to going away. Well, at that age it was all a bit of an adventure and we hadn't any idea what the war was going to be. The only thing that really terrified him was the thought of telling Mum and what her reaction would be.

At first he kept the call-up secret: he just didn't want her to know in case she got all emotional. Of course, she had to know and I eventually convinced him to tell her. But then, even more important, he refused point-blank to tell her when he was due to go.

'I don't want her blubbing all over the station, it'll show me up,' and so on. I said that he couldn't just go off on his own with no one to go with him to the station and, eventually, he agreed that I could go. I seemed to get all the 'going-to-the-station-to-say-goodbye' jobs. Anyway, Mum wasn't stupid and it was impossible for Bob to hide all his arrangements, so she soon worked out when he would be going. On the day she got up early, got herself ready, sat down in the kitchen and waited. When the time finally came to go she just stood there and insisted so that, in the end, Bob had to give in.

We had to walk up to Bow to catch the bus to the station; I can't remember what station he had to go from, but Bob was terribly embarrassed all the way. Fancy your mother crying over you as you went off to war. As we approached the bus stop there was a bus drawing in – not our one though – and we saw a man running up a side street for all he was worth. So Mum did no more than step out in front of the bus and tell the driver to wait. The bus driver told her, in pretty broad language, about his timetable and how he had to get to wherever by whatever, etc, etc. In return Mum told him, in just as broad language, about the pressures of wartime, being reasonable, giving people a chance, etc, etc. She would not be moved. Only when the fellow reached the end of the side street he turned left, ran straight past the bus, and headed off up the road to goodness knows where! Good God, that really started it and I thought the war would be coming to an end right there. By this stage Bob was totally beside himself with embarrassment and there was terror in his eyes as he thought ahead to the scene at the station.

Well, we reached the station and there was the platform – a whole mass of people, mainly young men going off to war and young women hugging, weeping, kissing. Not a mother to be seen anywhere. Poor Bob. But then we got the surprise. Mum didn't say or do anything, but as she stood there these girls seemed to gravitate towards her. In no time at all she was surrounded by them, giving a word of comfort here, a little smile there, a squeeze to another. She was the pillar of strength supporting all the sorrow and anxiety that was being piled up on that platform. Looking back, I realise that she had maturity, she represented life going on and, of course, she had experience because she had been through it all before in the First World War. She was the heroine of the hour, the star of the day, and we looked at her with new eyes.

A little later in the war my sister Tiny was working in a menswear shop and really quite liked it. Her best mate was named Marie and was ever so posh. She had, it turned out, been 'given away' soon after her birth because her mother just couldn't afford to bring her up. Instead she was brought up by her aunt who, it seems, looked after her quite well. For some reason, though, she was desperate to get away. At the time they began the call up for women, mainly into the Land Army and things like that, but they had concessions for those who volunteered. If girls volunteered and joined up together they could stay together and be posted 'near home'. So one day Marie started working on Tiny and suggested that they should join up together. After a bit Tiny agreed and they volunteered. Eventually the day came for them to leave. They went from Stratford station. So there we were, standing on the platform waiting for the

Bob (left) and an army colleague with their lorry.

train to start, when suddenly Marie's aunt/mother suddenly cried out to Tiny 'to look after my little girl'. This, for some reason, made Mum see red and she led off something chronic at this woman about who looked after who, whose idea it was, her poor child going 'off to the country' and goodness knows what else. It turned out later that Marie was desperate to get away because her aunt's 'boyfriend' had started to molest her. Still, Tiny and Marie had a great time together living in the country and it was while serving near Colchester that Tiny met her husband to be.

One day six of the Land Girls, including Tiny, were out hoeing in fields near Peldon when they heard a plane approaching. When they looked up they saw it was a Flying Fortress flying low, streaming smoke and obviously in a bad way. It finally ploughed into the ground a few fields away, so they all ran over to see what had happened and whether they could help. It was all a terrible mess, but lying on the ground a few yards from the wreck was an airman who seemed to be just a mass of burns. They were sure they had to do something but couldn't think what. Eventually, in desperation, Tiny rushed off to the edge of the field and lifted the gate off its hinges – goodness knows where she got the strength from. Then between them they carried the gate over to the man, lifted him onto it, and then carried him a couple of miles across the fields to the nearest main road.

That was that. They never heard any more, whether he lived or died, went back home or whatever. In wartime you didn't hear these things, it was all 'security'. They didn't even know the man's name, only that he was an American airman. The sequel came almost exactly fifty years later. Somebody saw an item in one of the local papers about an American ex-pilot trying to trace the girls who had saved his life all those years before. Knowing Tiny's story they told her about it and, after much umming and aahing, she contacted the address given. The local paper had taken up the cause and after much checking and chasing managed to trace five of the girls, including Tiny. Eventually the airman, now a retired US Air Force Colonel living in Spokane, Washington, came over and they had a reunion which made the national press and television.

Mind you, I don't think Tiny will ever forgive him for his admiring tribute to 'the Butch girl who lifted the gate off its hinges!' That was her. [Editor's note: A couple of years later Tiny was informed by the US Embassy in London of his death – she was very touched that they should have remembered her].

20

Produce

(1940–5)

Mum could cook a good meat-and-two-veg meal, even if it was a right performance and a terrible ordeal for everybody around her, but for everything else she was a real 'hit and miss' cook. The food could come out beautifully or it could be a disaster, there was no way of knowing in advance which it would be, and Mum didn't know either. One day in the war, though, when I called round to see her, she put on the table the most beautiful cake you had ever seen. It had the most perfect texture and yellow colour – it looked like a picture in a book.

'Have a piece,' she said, and set about cutting a great big slice. I just couldn't understand it. I mean, where could she have got the ingredients, especially the fat, because it was so tightly rationed? If you did manage to get enough fat together to make a cake you certainly didn't dish it out in big slices. There was something going on.

'Where did you get the fat from?' I asked.

'Just have a piece and enjoy it,' she replied, 'it's ever so good.'

'Yes, but where did you get the fat from?' I repeated.

After another couple of rounds of this to-and-fro she finally said it was from the butcher. Well, that was no answer because fat from the butcher was on ration just like everything else, so there still had to be more to it. I kept on asking and asking, and refusing to take a slice of cake, until I got the truth. Eventually she

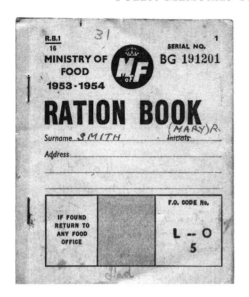

*Polly's final ration book,
kept just in case . . .*

admitted that it was horse-fat, which accounted for the beautiful colour of the cake! Well, you know how horse fat is quite yellow. It seems that the butcher had managed to get hold of a supply and then found that he couldn't sell it. Even with the tight rationing nobody would buy horse-fat until Mum turned up and took the lot for a knock-down price. I am afraid that even for a knock-down price I still couldn't bring myself to eat horse so I never did taste the cake. I don't even know what happened to it and whether anybody else ate it.

These sorts of things seemed to happen to Mum. I remember that she was no good at making tea and somehow she never cracked the problem. Whenever she made tea it tasted awful and generally we used to avoid it, which suited her down to the ground because tea was expensive. Once, though, early in the war, I went round to see her and she was ever so insistent that I should have a cup of tea. I was suspicious and eventually got it out of her that she had got it cheap from 'that man up the road.' Well, 'that man up the road' was a real spiv. Goodness knows where he got his stuff from, but it must have been pinched. Everything he sold was ex-army and dirt cheap; he sold new army blankets for 4s at one time, I remember. Anyway, Mum had bought this tea from him and, because it was so cheap she had bought a load of it and was feeling generous. When I eventually gave in and said that I would have some tea she proudly went and got a packet out from the cupboard under the end of the dresser. She boiled the kettle, looking ever so smug, and made the tea. I was dreading it because, as I said, Mum couldn't make tea. In the event it was worse than you could have ever imagined in your worst dream – even Mum couldn't drink it! Unfortunately the taste was all too obvious and the reason all too clear. Mum had also bought a large quantity of cheap, almost certainly ex-army (if the army had ever managed to get its hands on it, that is), carbolic soap and she had stacked the whole of this treasure trove together under the dresser. She tried separating them but it was no good because the damage had already been done. After a couple of weeks she had to throw all the tea away – a fine bargain that turned out to be.

Later in the war we were evacuated to Six Mile Bottom, about halfway between Cambridge and Newmarket. Our Jane was out there with the Land Army and she fixed it all up for me. We stayed with 'Aunty Blinco' in one of six terraced farm cottages, which stood alone at the end of a long tree-lined drive coming up from the main road. It was in the middle of nowhere. It was just like the romantic idea of a cottage, with two rooms downstairs and two up. The floors were made of brick, but until very recently they had still been dirt. The ceilings were low, you stooped to go through a door, and the staircase was almost a ladder in the corner of the front room. Water came from a pump outside and the garden looked like a 'cottage garden' illustration on the box of a jigsaw puzzle.

Aunty had her own story to tell. She had married young and soon had a small family. Disaster struck when her husband died, leaving her to be the youngest widow anybody in the area could ever remember. She had no means of support apart from a tiny plot of land but she was a worker and set-to, just so that she and the kids could survive. She used the plot of land to grow onions and sold them locally. She got just about enough money each year to scrape through to the next. Eventually she remarried, and after that life was much easier. 'Uncle' was much younger than her, but they were a devoted couple and lived out a long life together. He was a farm worker on the estate, which was how they came to be living in one of the estate cottages. He worked long hours on the estate and when he got home from there he would work more hours in the garden growing their vegetables. He used to go out once a week, regular as clockwork, every Saturday night down to the pub with his mates.

One Saturday, as he was going out, he mentioned that he might bring back some greengages – his friend, 'A', had said he would let him have a basketful. Aunty hit the roof!

'There is absolutely no way I am going to have his greengages in the house!'
'But they are free and will bottle well – make jam!'
'That doesn't matter, there are none of his greengages coming into this house!'
'Well it seems silly to waste them, and they are good ones . . .'
'That's even worse, if they come back I will leave home . . .'
They carried on to and fro like this for at least a quarter of an hour until

Uncle gave in and left for the pub. I was terribly embarrassed, because I had never seen Uncle and Aunty argue like that and I didn't know what to say. So I just kept my mouth shut and tried to avoid the subject, but in the end, Aunty told me anyway. Apparently 'A' and his wife lived in one of the cottages over at somewhere or other. His wife was always pregnant and must have had a baby every year, but never did they have a child. Of course, out in those remote areas you never got a midwife and I don't suppose they could have afforded one anyway. Come to that, they couldn't have afforded any extra mouths to feed either. Whether those two facts were related or just coincidence I don't know, but every year another baby went under that greengage tree – and there was no way on God's earth that Aunty was going to eat the fruit that came off it! It was just another sign of how rough life could be out in the remote country areas in the first half of the century.

It was amazing to hear what went on. I remember once talking to an older lady who was dreadfully sad about how she had no family. She was ever so vague though, and I couldn't really make sense of the bits of stories and hints she was giving me. So I just agreed with her and sympathised. When I got back to the cottage I asked Aunty about her. It took Aunty a little while to work out who I was talking about, but then she told me the story. Her husband used to be head gardener up at the big house and they had quite a good little family. But then one winter one of the children caught diphtheria and in no time all the kids had caught it. Eventually they had to call the doctor in and his only advice was that the children had to be kept warm and cosy. That was much easier said than done, especially living in a small, unheated estate cottage and eventually, in desperation, the father made up beds for the children in one of the heated greenhouses and nursed them there. It is amazing to think that they could heat greenhouses but not homes for sick children, and nobody thought that it was at all unreasonable! Anyway, it was all to no avail and one-by-one the children died. Of course, you couldn't keep that sort of thing quiet and slowly the story came out. When the master heard about it he was livid – children dying is one thing but up at the house they ate food that had been grown in those greenhouses. He promptly had the greenhouses burnt down and sacked the father. Of course, that was a real disaster in those days and though he did his best to make a living he soon gave up the struggle and died young. His wife never really recovered her wits and was always a bit touched, unsurprisingly. The master and his wife went down on the *Titanic*, but I don't think anybody was too upset.

21

Doodlebugs and Rockets

(1944–5)

After the Blitz things went a bit quiet until near the end of the war, when we got the doodlebugs and rockets. We were living in Keogh Road and I already had a great big lump, expecting my second boy. By then doodlebugs were getting a bit routine so we always used to sleep in the Morrison shelter, with a piano between us and the window for extra protection. I made a small bag out of a bit of spare cloth and every night I packed this with a towel, some water, a baby's bottle and a sandwich, and I used to put this in the shelter 'just in case' of emergencies. Well, this night the warning went and so I hurriedly packed the bag and put it, and the baby (well, he was more of a toddler by then), in the shelter. Fred, of course, was already down at the warden post. He used to work all day, be at the post all night, then just come in for breakfast before going to work again. God knows how he kept it up.

My brother George had been visiting us that night but had left to go home and I had done various odd jobs before getting ready for bed. Nearly an hour later there was a knock on the door and there stood George. Now George suffered from night blindness, in fact he couldn't see a thing in the dark. He hadn't been gone long when the warning went and, of course, they turned off all the lights. There wasn't much light to find your way around at the best of times, but in a raid there was none and poor old George was totally blind.

It seems that he had wandered round in circles for ages, trying to recognise something or somewhere by feel. Some fellow had asked him where Keogh Road was, but George couldn't help because he didn't know where he was! At least, though, he now had a companion in his search. Anyway, they then found somebody else who gave them directions and so the second fellow was able to bring George back to our house. I was dumbstruck to see him on the doorstep, but then the warden from somewhere shouted about closing down the light from the door and so I pulled him inside.

It was obvious that he wasn't going home that night so he stayed with me. I suppose he could have come into the shelter but it didn't seem quite right to me so he went upstairs to the spare bed. It was late summer and ever so warm, besides which he didn't have any pyjamas with him anyway, so he slept in the nude. The next morning I was sort of woken up by Fred's voice, far away, shouting to 'stay in the shelter!' I didn't quite take it in, and promptly climbed out of the shelter. Suddenly WHUMMMPHT – the world started shaking, bits

Ref: A.R.P./Voucher.

The Grand Priory in the British Realm
of the
Uenerable Order of the Hospital of St. John of Jerusalem
AMBULANCE DEPARTMENT.

The St. John Ambulance Brigade.

Chief Commissioner :
Major-General SIR JOHN DUNCAN, K.C.B., C.M.G., C.V.O., D.S.O.

This is to Certify that

FREDERICK F. SMITH

has been re-examined for the————First————year in AIR RAID

PRECAUTIONS AND FIRST AID FOR AIR RAID CASUALTIES, and

satisfied the Examiner.

28th March. 1942.   Air Raid Precautions Commissioner.

One of Fred's (many) ARP training certificates.

A letter of commendation for Fred's handling of the Keogh Road incident.

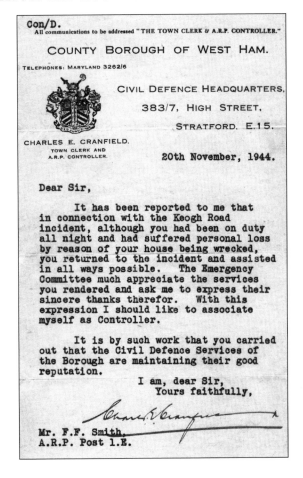

Con/D.

All communications to be addressed "THE TOWN CLERK & A.R.P. CONTROLLER."

COUNTY BOROUGH OF WEST HAM.

TELEPHONES: MARYLAND 3262/6

CIVIL DEFENCE HEADQUARTERS,

383/7, HIGH STREET,

STRATFORD. E.15.

CHARLES E. CRANFIELD.
TOWN CLERK AND
A.R.P. CONTROLLER.

20th November, 1944.

Dear Sir,

It has been reported to me that in connection with the Keogh Road incident, although you had been on duty all night and had suffered personal loss by reason of your house being wrecked, you returned to the incident and assisted in all ways possible. The Emergency Committee much appreciate the services you rendered and ask me to express their sincere thanks therefor. With this expression I should like to associate myself as Controller.

It is by such work that you carried out that the Civil Defence Services of the Borough are maintaining their good reputation.

I am, dear Sir,
Yours faithfully,

Mr. F.F. Smith,
A.R.P. Post 1.E.

of the house fell in, there were clouds of plaster everywhere and I didn't know whether I was on my head or my feet. At which moment George appeared, stark naked.

I got Fred's side of the story later. Having spent the night at the post he was on his way home for breakfast when the warning went again. This time it was a doodlebug coming our way and that was when he had to run the last few yards home, screaming to me to stay put and waking me up in the process. It had just passed over when the engine cut out, but for some reason it didn't carry straight on but turned and came back again diving straight towards him. Looking back it was just plain stupid, but at the time Fred could think of nothing better to do than lift his arms up to catch the thing and stop it hitting the ground! He said he felt that he could almost touch it and always remembered its great shadow passing over him. It landed just a few houses away, but somehow we were sheltered from the very worst of the blast. Needless to say it killed the couple in the house where it landed. We had always thought that they were brother and sister but it emerged from all the fuss that they were an unmarried couple living together; quite a scandal then but nobody had suspected anything.

Of course, Fred was the senior person on site and as soon as he saw that I was alright he went back to the post and immediately took control. He set up his control post and in no time at all was busy organising rescues here, cars there, checking for people trapped in ruins, clearing the street and all the rest. Truth be told, he was in his element organising things, but he did do a marvellous job. In fact, he later got an official Letter of Commendation from the Borough ARP Controller for the exemplary work he had done in the situation, despite his own home being among those wrecked in the incident.

Anyway, back home, George was standing there stark naked in the rubble of our front room. He too had heard Fred shouting and was rushing downstairs to tell me to stay put when the bomb went off. I found an old sheet and tore it in half so he could wrap it around himself and then he gingerly cleared a way up what remained of the staircase – and it wasn't very much – to the ruin of the bedroom. He managed to find his clothes and got dressed, though he looked a bit of a shambles. I then got Robert out of the shelter and we went out in the street and sat on a low wall. I could see Fred up the road surrounded by loads of people and doing his organising. I was happy to leave him to it, when along came a nurse.

Polly's casualty card.

'You're injured,' she said.

'No I'm not,' I replied.

'Yes you are,' she said.

And, sure enough, I had some sort of cut at the top of my nose and the blood was trickling down my face. I couldn't feel anything, I think because apart from the shock I was absolutely covered in plaster-dust and it was just soaking up the blood as it went. So she wrote a label, pinned it on me, and said I had to go to hospital. Then we had another performance because I said that I couldn't leave the baby, and it was quite clear that Fred couldn't look after him. Luckily Mrs Jones from a couple of doors along came up at that point and she took Robert.

Then I had to go and see Fred who, as controller, whistled up a car from nowhere and off I went to Forest Lane Hospital. This was a maternity hospital really, but in those days anybody would deal with anything. I suppose they had to. They cleaned up the wound very quickly and it turned out to be pretty trivial, but the doctor patted me on the tummy and asked when it was due. When I told him he decided that I would have to stay in for observation, so we had another performance while I told him about the other baby. Eventually he said I would have to take some pill or other, and then he would let me out if I promised to take it easy.

While I was waiting I got talking to this old lady who was waiting for transport. She had been injured but was a bit unhinged too, and truth be told had no idea what was going on. They had found somewhere for her to go and now she had to wait. Eventually my pill turned up, and I swear it was the size of a tennis ball. I have never been good at taking pills and goodness knows how many attempts it took before I finally got this one down. No sooner had I done so when a taxi arrived. I decided to be helpful, so I went and found the old lady and packed her into the taxi, then set out to walk back home. After about a hundred yards I heard all this shouting, and looked round to see the doctor and a couple of nurses running down the road after me. The taxi was for me, not the old lady.

When I got back there wasn't much to be done. The house was ruined and so dangerous that it would have to be pulled down as soon as possible. Fred was still organising the recovery crews who were, by now, salvaging whatever furniture could be saved and arranging for it to go into store. I was given a ticket for Salway School where there was an emergency shelter and arrangements for feeding those who had been bombed out. As I was leaving this soldier came running out of the ruins of the house and held out his hand.

With Hearty Congratulations
and wishing you unitedly
much happiness in your
Wedded Life
From The Kellys.

Mrs Kelly's purse and contents.

'Is this yours, missus?' he asked.

He was holding the purse that Mrs Kelly had given us as a wedding present. It contained our 10s. 10s was a lot of money when Mrs Kelly had given it to us and we had decided to keep it for emergencies. In a real emergency it would have bought us a week's food, or paid the rent, or just tided us over. We got very close to using it once or twice in the early days, but never quite needed it. Whenever the design of notes was changed we substituted one of the new ones, but otherwise we hung onto it – and I have still got it complete with the little gift card from Mrs Kelly. It was still a lot of money even then and I have always remembered the honesty of that soldier – he could easily have kept that money and nobody would have ever been any the wiser. I suppose war brings out the best in some people, just like it brings out the worst in others.

Anyway, I arranged to go and stay with my sister in Buckhurst Hill and Fred arranged a car to take us there. My sister Jane was in the Land Army near Newmarket, and she found me a billet in a little hamlet nearby. That was how we'd met Aunty Blinco.

While we were away Fred found us half a requisitioned house in Earlham Grove, just round the corner from Keogh Road. We might have been safe in the country, but I didn't want to risk having my second baby with the primitive hospital system there, so when it was due I wanted to return to London.

Fred wasn't happy with the idea and tried to talk me out of it – he even sent me a letter listing all the incidents during a 3-day period but I still thought that London-with-bombs was safer than the Newmarket local hospitals (see chapter 18). By then the doodlebugs had finished, but we were getting rockets instead. They were worse because you got no warning and there was nothing you could do. One day I was walking down Earlham Grove with Robert in the pushchair and little Keith Lee walking beside me. He was a friend of Robert's and I had taken the pair of them shopping. As we crossed Sprowston Road we were suddenly lifted about 2ft off the ground – all three of us – and then put down again. Almost immediately there was an almighty explosion at the other end of Earlham Grove where the rocket fell. I have never heard anybody else talk about it, but I am sure there must have been some sort of air-wave or something as the rocket went past.

A mother and her child were killed in that incident. This woman and her husband were a bit strange, in fact I think that they were rather simple. Their son was an absolute horror and everybody used to avoid him and keep their kids away from him, but his parents loved him and they were such a happy little family. For some reason, though, the son and Robert really hit it off and they used to play together ever such a lot. An hour or so after the rocket landed I was standing at the door and saw the father walking down the road. He had been called at work and told of the deaths. As he walked down the road the tears were just rolling down his face – I can still see him and it still chokes me up to think about it.

At the very end of the war I was just coming out of Woolworths with Robert (and the baby in the pram) as a man was coming in. He looked at us and fainted! He was a manager in the sugar-boiling department at Clarnico when I used to work there and he lived nearby when we were in Keogh Road. Robert used to hang on the gate watching the world go by, so this man first used to say hello, then he talked to Robert, then used to give him a sweet, and eventually Robert asked if he could have a sweet for his Mum too, so he used to get two sweets. This man had thought that it was me and Robert who had been killed by the rocket – no wonder he fainted.

The other near-miss was the rocket that landed in the middle of Earlham Grove. We were away at the time and it only did minor damage to the house, including shaking most of the plaster off the living room wall. When Jane got married just after the war we covered the gap with a huge Union Jack. That rocket provided the site for Earlham Grove School.

22

Early Post-War

(1945–50)

It's funny to look back to just after the war and remember how rough it was, though at the time we thought that it was fine – I suppose because it was so different from the war. Really, anything was bound to be good when you weren't being bombed and didn't have to worry about who was going to get killed next. The council gave us half a requisitioned house in Earlham Grove. Goodness knows who had owned it before or how it came to be requisitioned but at the time you just didn't think about that sort of thing. It was one of those big Edwardian houses with big rooms and tall ceilings, and was built for an altogether more gracious age. It even had a coach house. Well, we called it the garage but it was meant for a horse and carriage. It was built onto the side of the house and had huge double doors to allow the carriage to go in and out but, of course, we only ever used the little wicket gate let into one corner of one of the big doors. It even had a hayloft, to keep food for the horse I suppose, but we never went up there. The house must have been built early in the century when that area of Forest Gate was the choice of wealthy Jews from the East End rag trade who moved out to be away from the squalor but in easy reach of their factories. There were still a lot of Jews living along there and next door the Bs still even had a maid. She was a leftover from the 1920s when the middle classes all had a live-in maid, but Annie (that was her name) had never moved on and became pretty well one of the family. Goodness knows

Polly's two sons in the garden of Earlham Grove in about 1948.

how old she was, but by then I think she needed more help from the family than she could ever give them.

The upstairs half of our house was given to Mr and Mrs J who had lived just along by us in Keogh Road. They had one son named Reggie who was a teenager by then. Mind you, in those days we had never heard of teenagers; you just grew up from being a child to being an adult. Anyway, we had the downstairs half, which had a front room, a large kitchen in the middle, and a back room which opened through a conservatory into the garden. Our half of the house included the cellar, with its huge old stone wash-boiler in one corner, heated by lighting a fire under it, and the loo in the opposite corner. It also had a separate front cellar, which was once used by the maid but was now just an odds and ends store of stuff from whoever used to live there before us. Upstairs we used the front room as the bedroom, with our double bed in the middle and the boys' beds in opposite corners on either side of us. The back room was rather grand and had obviously been the lounge, but it cost a fortune to heat so it was usually very cold and we didn't use it much apart from high days and holidays. I remember that when we moved in the walls were covered in some awful smelling brown-stain that had obviously trickled down the wall. I think it must have been disinfectant or something. I suppose that says something about the state of the place before it was requisitioned but it didn't bother us – we were just pleased to get a roof over our heads. It took ages to scrub it all off though, and even then I could always smell it but nobody else did. Maybe it was just my imagination. Our George slept in that room for a while when he was first de-mobbed and before he got himself settled down. But to all intents and purposes we lived in the kitchen, with its huge dresser all along one wall, a big pine kitchen table in the middle and a couple of easy chairs beside the fire. We only lived there for a few years, but we had some happy times and I still think of that as our first real home, perhaps because that was the first place where we had both boys and the family was 'complete'. It wasn't at all convenient and for baths we had to use a tin-bath in front of the fire – though heating water was such a pain we didn't use it very much (Fred used to take himself up to the Turkish Baths once a week).

Just after the war we still had rationing, but even when stuff was off-ration nothing was easy to come by and you had to make do. One year we decided to raise some chickens for eggs and meat and so we went down to the egg-and-chick shop in Angel Lane and bought some day-old chicks. You could actually buy day-old chicks from this shop – it had a wooden box display in the window heated by a light bulb and it was always full of little fluffy chicks. The boys used to be fascinated. Anyway, we bought these chicks and though some of them died pretty quickly we managed to raise a couple of them in the shed at the end of the garden. We didn't have much success with the eggs so we decided that it was time to try the meat but, of course, this meant we had to kill one of them and we realised for the first time that none of us quite knew how. Well, we knew how, but none of us had the confidence to actually do it without causing the poor creature to suffer. At last my brother Bob volunteered to wring its neck and then, of course, we were all full of advice about how it should be done – how you had to be firm and do it quickly and strongly. The eldest boy was always a bit soft-hearted about animals and had got quite attached to the chickens so we had to send him off on some errand or something and Bob went to get the chicken. He brought it down to the garage and stood there holding the poor blighter while we all watched. At last he said that he couldn't do it while we were watching so we all went inside and waited. Suddenly there was this awful cry of, 'Mary! Mary!' from the garage so we all rushed out to see what could possibly have happened. And there was poor Bob, standing there as white as a sheet, holding the chicken's head in one hand while this headless chicken was running round and round his feet. He was absolutely stuck to the ground in terror and we were just as paralysed with laughing, until the poor thing fell down. Afterwards he told us that he was so concerned about not making the poor thing suffer that he had wound his arms round as far as he could with his hands round the chicken's neck and then untwisted them round as hard and as fast as he could, but so hard and fast that its head had come clean off! We just had time to clean up the mess and hide the evidence before the eldest boy got back and we told him that somebody had stolen the chicken. I don't know whether he ever put two and two together when we had chicken for dinner.

Talking about having to make do, I remember when Reggie brought home his first girlfriend and Mrs J was ever so keen to impress her. Well, you couldn't get proper toilet paper and most people, like us, just used squares of newspaper. Cutting up newspapers was a regular household job. Anyway, on this occasion Mrs J was ever so proud of herself because she managed to get hold of some air-mail paper. It might not have been proper toilet paper, but it was definitely a class better than newspaper. Sure enough, Reggie brought his girlfriend home and everybody was on their best behaviour, until Reggie went to the loo. A few minutes later he returned with a smirk all over his face.

'Mother,' he said, 'I know things are tight, but are we really reduced to this?' And he held up a sheet of the air-mail toilet paper with clearly written across the bottom, 'Please Use Both Sides.'

You had to admire the Js. They were real working class, but understood the value of education and were determined to do their very best for Reggie. He eventually got a place at Reading University and they moved heaven and earth to support him through it; not an easy job in the days before grants. You could see them getting shabbier and shabbier as the days went by, but supporting Reggie was the number one priority and they really stuck to it. When he finished he got a job with that Harwell place, something to do with atomic power. They moved away in the late 1940s, to High Wycombe I think, and eventually we lost touch but I have always wondered what happened to them.

The garage was quite useful because it was outside, but closed off from the road and under cover, so we could do any messy jobs out there and the boys could play there any time. The youngest boy used to love it because he was always into 'making things' and would sit out there for hours with some scraps of wood, a hammer and some nails, and just knock things together. He always knew what he was making, though it was honestly not always obvious to anybody else. For him, though, the garage was a smashing workshop and whenever I took him shopping we used to call in at Woolworths and get a quarter of nails – he would rather have nails than sweets – and he would then spend the rest of the day out in the garage. Of course, the boys were never fussy about the lock on the little wicket gate and used to run in and out without bothering and would leave it unlocked or even open. Fred used to get ever so worried about this and the danger of burglars so he used to make a performance about telling us to check it every night after the boys came in, or checking it himself if he was around. One night, though, he was coming home from work very late and decided to teach us a lesson by creeping in through the back and surprising us all in the kitchen. So as to heighten the surprise he didn't turn the light on in the garage and crept through in the dark as quietly as he could until, that is, he stepped on a piece of wood with half a dozen nails hammered through it! He let out the most enormous yell and came hopping into the kitchen screaming blue murder about leaving such dangerous things lying around. As soon as he realised what was going on, the youngest boy also started screaming blue murder about his dad wrecking his model of a boat. I don't know how we managed to keep them apart, but we never heard any more about security and the side door.

The only trouble with Earlham Grove is that it was a long way from any schools and the boys had a long way to walk each day, especially as they didn't like school dinners and so came home to lunch. About a year before we moved away they built a new school just up the road on the site where the V2 had fallen right at the end of the war and the youngest boy went there for a short while. I don't think they were very pleased with him though. It was one of those terribly modern schools where they believed in all that self-expression stuff and also that children had to be happy in order to learn. I suppose it was all very advanced at the time and the school was treated as a showpiece with all sorts of special visitors. Well, one day I got a note asking me to go up to the school and discuss our son's progress. It quite shocked me because when I was a child your parents never had anything to do with school and I couldn't think what was terrible enough to need a parent to be called to see the headmistress. When I arrived they sent for my son and in we went to see the headmistress. It turned out that they had had some 'important visitor' who had addressed the class and asked who was happy at school. All the hands went up, except one. So he tried the opposite tack and asked who wasn't happy at school, and this time just one hand went up. This was such a disaster they sent for me to discuss the problems. They went through our home conditions, family background, and all that stuff – in fact, I thought they were very nosey – but still couldn't find any reason why the boy didn't like school. Eventually they asked him, and he just said that he would rather be at home making things so after that they used to let him take a hammer and nails to school and he used to sit in the corner of the classroom 'making things'. He didn't stay there much longer because we moved to the other side of Stratford, but when he got to his new school his teacher could only say that she had never known a child who was so bright but didn't know anything!

I must say that the Jews were ever so good about the children. They really loved them and were ever so kind. When the youngest was born I took him straight in next door to show him off. I was a bit shocked because they were having some sort of party and had lots of visitors. I tried to leave again but they would have none of it – instead they took the baby off me and he was passed around the room from hand to hand with lots of oohs and aahs. Several of them muttered over him in some language I didn't understand – I suppose it was Hebrew. It got me quite worried after a while and I began to imagine all sorts of dark curses but he turned out alright so perhaps they were blessings! One Mother's Day, when he was about five or so, he went into their garden and picked all their daffodils to give to me as a present. When I realised what had happened I wanted to wring his neck but they thought it was ever so thoughtful of him and managed to restrain me. They even gave him some leftover pieces of smoked salmon but I am afraid I ate them and told him the cat had pinched it. I think I earned it.

One of his friends up the street was the boy Collins. He had some 'illness' – I think he was a diabetic – and the family were always ever so anxious about him. He was very rarely let out to play and they were always going on about the dangers of him cutting himself. However, he sometimes came to play with the kids in our garden. There were some old paint tins in the corner of the garage left by whoever had been there before us. Imagine my horror one day to find Collins and our youngest without their shirts on carefully rubbing grey paint all over their bodies. I must say, he was never allowed down to us again! Not that it did any good because he died a couple of years later and it cast a real cloud over our end of the street for ages.

The youngest boy's best friend was Martin, a Jewish boy who lived a few doors up the street. They were about the same age, but Martin had a baby brother. My boy seemed to spend most of the time up there, certainly a lot more time than he ever spent at home, but he always came home for his meals.

Martin's mother was really upset about this and got herself quite worked up. She even came to see me to say how much she wished he would stay and have a meal with them but nothing she could say would ever persuade him to stay. I said that I didn't mind at all if he stayed so I would try to find out what was the problem. One day, I raised the subject with him as gently as I could but he wasn't at all bothered. He just looked at me and asked 'Have you seen Martin's baby? He wears his dressing gown all day and he dribbles. I don't want to eat anything near him!' I was amazed. I never thought that he could be that fussy, but after that 'Martin's baby' became the family code for any messy eater, food-spill, dirty clothes, or the like.

23

The Fog

(1950–1)

You don't have fogs now like we used to in London. Well, they weren't fog, were they? They were that awful smog, full of all the smoke from the fires in them. At the time we did not realise just how bad they were – in fact, nobody did but it is good that all this clean air law and stuff has sorted it all out. The kids used to get sent home from school early at least once a year because it was just too dangerous to be out. Well, I suppose the truth is that the teachers wanted to get home while there were still some buses around. It could truly get so bad that everything – cars, buses, trains, the lot – just stopped.

I can remember one really bad night when I had gone over to see Ted. Now, after Dad died Mum had to get a job and at the factory she met this bloke Ted. He was only a watchman or gatekeeper or something, but they got on ever so well and eventually she married him. All told they only had a couple of years together but I think Mum was happier than ever she had been with Dad. They had a little house with a bay window and sometimes they would put a chair each in either side of the bay, make a couple of sandwiches and just sit there and watch the world go by. Once a week he used to take her to the pictures as well – my Dad never took her anywhere. I think she really was happy with him. Anyway, after she died I used to carry on visiting Ted and keeping an eye on him. He was a nice old boy; I can't remember what he died of in the end.

Anyway, this evening I went over to see him. Fred had some swimming meeting or other and he would be out until late so young George was babysitting the boys. It was a bit foggy when I went out but after I had spent an hour or so with Ted it had turned into a real pea-souper. And I mean a pea-souper – if you held your hand out at arms length you could not see it! Well, I was not going to stay at Ted's, and anyway, I had lived in Stratford all my life so I knew the place like the back of my hand. I really did not need to be able to see to find my way home. No chance of a bus, of course, so I set out to walk.

You could not see the ground, but I knew where the kerbs were, and all the side-roads, so I could just keep count as I made my way along. My plan was to get to the Broadway, because the kerb there was so high that it had been made into a double step. I thought that it would give me a check on where I was and also tell me where to cross the road. The church was on a huge traffic island in the middle of the road so there was one-way traffic round it, and that would make it easier to keep an eye open for any traffic because it would all be coming from the same direction. Not that there would be anything out and about in that fog. The other advantage with crossing in the Broadway was that it put me on the right side of the road to go straight down Romford Road without trying to sort out the road junction around Young & Martens. It was a bit complicated there. So, you see, I had it all worked out.

Well, when I reckoned I had reached the Broadway I carefully stepped down the kerb and, sure enough, there was the double step. So I carefully stepped down again but it was much deeper than I ever remembered and I went absolutely sprawling. I suppose by instinct I jumped straight back up and turned round quickly to see if there was any traffic. Of course there was not, and if there had been it would have got me anyway. But by then I had absolutely no idea where I was. I had completely lost all sense of direction and could not even see the road under my feet, let alone know where the kerb was that I had just left. It put the wind up me something rotten, but I had to do something so I slowly headed off forward, not really knowing where I was going. Eventually I came to a kerb, which was a great relief, and I got back onto a pavement. But where? I decided the best thing was to try to find the buildings on the other side of the pavement, and because this time I knew where the line of the pavement was I set off at right angles to it.

I was slowly feeling my way forward when I came to some railings. That absolutely floored me, because there were only shops in the Broadway, no railings anywhere. I felt my way up and down them. They had fancy tops on the spikes so I brought my eyes ever so close up until I could just about see them in the gloom. Then I realised, they were the railings around Elizabeth Fry's statue in The Grove. Well, that was a long way from where I thought I was, but it gave me a point of reference again so I was able to set off, knowing exactly where I was and what I was doing. I don't know exactly what she had done for prisoners and prison reform, but Elizabeth Fry saved my life that night!

From there on it was fairly straightforward for a bit, because Romford Road was just long and straight. I knew all the side roads so I could work out where I was, and because of the mix-up in the Broadway I was now on the right side of the road for getting home and would not have to cross over again. I had to pass the Conservative Club and thought that Fred would probably be in there by now, but decided not to go in to find him. It would mean crossing the road again and even then would take a bit of effort to find the club, at the end of which Fred would only tell me off for going out on such a rotten night. I am not sure that he altogether approved of Ted anyway. So I pressed on.

Eventually I reached Atherton Road and turned down it. For some reason I didn't feel nearly so confident down here, perhaps because it was not a main road, so I felt more 'alone' even though I hadn't seen anybody else all the way home. I decided to cross at the top of the road and then walk along the kerb until I reached the pillar box. From there I would be able to work out the corner of Earlham Grove, which otherwise wasn't very simple. I had just reached the pillar box, and was taking a bit of a breather to get ready for the last stretch home when a voice came out of the dark.

'Is there somebody there?' it asked.

'Yes,' I replied, 'Where are you?'

'I don't really know. I am looking for Atherton Road.'

'Well, you have found it, but where are you looking for?'

It turned out that she was a midwife who had been called out to an emergency. She thought she knew the area and the house well enough, but this fog had completely caught her out. Not surprising really; I walked this way home most days of my life but I wasn't feeling at all happy about finding my way.

'Well, hang on,' I said. 'I will just keep talking and you come towards me until you find the pillar box. Then you can find your way from here.' And that was what she did. Eventually she said she had found the box and we felt our way round it until we touched hands. I checked the address with her again and realised that she was looking for one of the larger houses a bit further down on the other side of the street. So I told her that she would have to cross straight over, turn right, and then find the house a bit further down. She assured me that this was OK, and off she went again. I waited for a bit and then called out

A Swimming Club dinner in the 1950s – just one of Fred's social engagements. Fred is standing third from left and Polly is sitting in front of him. Chrissie (p. 67) stands second from left, Milly sits first from left, while Lucy (see p. 67) sits first from the right.

to see if she was OK. Yes, she replied, she had got over and was just about to head off along the garden fences. So I decided it was time for me to go too, and from there I fairly quickly found my way home.

You know, I have had that woman on my conscience ever since. I never even saw her face, but I have always wondered whether she found her emergency and whether she found it in time. The houses on the other side of Atherton were all rather big, with big front gardens, so even if she found a gate it would be a difficult job finding the front door. There was no way of knowing what number you were at. To be honest, by then I was quite exhausted with the strain and I just couldn't face crossing a road again so I left her to find her own way. But I have always wondered.

It turned out that Fred had been in the club when I passed. His swimming meeting had finished quite early so he invited Milly up to the club for a drink. Milly was one of the other swimming club officials and, I think, she was always a bit soft on Fred. Anyway, while they were in the club the fog came down and by the time they left it was completely undriveable. Milly would have had trouble finding her car, let alone driving it. There was nothing for it and Fred had to invite her home to stay the night. I didn't usually stay up for Fred to get in, he could be very late sometimes. Next morning, when I got up, there was Milly in our lounging chair with a blanket over her! She was terribly sorry and all that and kept trying to say how bad the fog had been. She didn't have to tell me because I had been out in it, but I let her keep on apologising.

24

The Flats

(1952–6)

At Earlham Grove Mrs J had the upstairs half and we had downstairs and the cellar. It had very large rooms and they could be a pain to keep warm. The big problem, though, was that there weren't enough of them. We had a front parlour, which was used as the bedroom for the whole family, the kitchen in the middle which was used as a family living room, and at the back of the house was the sitting room. It was quite a grand room really, with a conservatory into the garden on the back, but it was expensive and difficult to heat so we didn't use it much. There was a separate toilet down in the cellar, and for a bath we used a tin-tub in front of the kitchen fire. When we first moved in the house had been used as a furniture store – I suppose for storing stuff recovered from bombed-out houses and the like. Probably some of it was none too clean, or maybe the council was taking no risks, but it was obvious that everything had been sprayed with insecticide and disinfectant. Perhaps we should be grateful because it certainly meant that there were no creepy-crawlies in there.

Anyway, it wasn't very satisfactory us all sleeping in the same room, especially when the oldest boy went to grammar school, so we kept pestering the council to get us rehoused but they didn't seem very interested at all. I remember going down to the council offices one day and the girl behind the counter read me the riot act. She told me all about how lucky we were to have a roof over our heads, and at least we had a separate bedroom, and we had a toilet, and we had a garden, and we shouldn't be greedy, and we ought to realise that other people had problems, and our children were only small (Robert was eleven or twelve by then) and on and on. I felt about half-an-inch tall by the time she finished with me and decided that I would never again go there to ask. Which was funny, because the next week we got a letter to say we were being rehoused to a modern, purpose-built flat in Stratford. It sounded really good, but looking back, that must be the worst place we ever lived.

The flat was the top corner of a block of six – three floors high and two flats on each floor, either side of a central staircase. The block had a flat roof, so our flat had three outside walls and a flat concrete slab roof. On top of that, it faced straight down a long wind tunnel of a road. It really was the coldest place on God's earth. In the winter we used to wake up to ice on the windows ¼in thick. In the living room we arranged the sofa and an armchair tightly around the fire with the television making the fourth side of the square, and that was the only comfortable place in the flat. Even walking over to the window was like walking into a fridge. At least we had two bedrooms so that the boys could have their own room. There were three other, larger blocks of flats and they were arranged as sides of a large courtyard that we called 'the Square', though I suppose that really it was a rectangle.

Opposite us on the top floor, just across the landing, was Mrs H. She was a funny woman, and full of airs and graces. We used to call her 'the Queen', ever since she told us that although it was a small flat, they had done it up like a palace and everybody who visited said how wonderful it was. Not that we ever saw many people visit. She would also tell anybody who cared to listen that she had married below her station. Her husband and daughter were both quiet and pleasant, but very much dominated by the Queen.

I never got her full story, or rather, I got so many stories that I was never sure which one was true. She had an older daughter who didn't live with her but came to visit very occasionally. Mrs H said that the girl's father was a rich Jew who was also a famous fighter pilot in the war, but as a Jew 'his people' wouldn't let him marry her. I don't know. Towards the end of the war she had met Mr H when he was serving in the army near Great Yarmouth somewhere. They, in turn, had to get married and that was their daughter, S. The Queen had a sister who visited on very rare occasions. Once she came when the Queen was out. She was knocking on the door as I was coming in, so I told her that Mrs H was out – 'What, looking for another man I suppose,'

Fred and Polly outside the flats in about 1955.

was her only response. I don't know what lay behind the remark but I guess it meant something about the background story.

Once when I came in from shopping the door was open and I could hear sobbing inside. I was a bit worried so I stood at the door and called in to ask if everything was all right. The sobbing got louder and more panic-stricken. I called again and it got worse again. So I put down my shopping and gingerly went in, calling out all the while. I soon found S in the small bedroom, laying on her bed all bloodstained and sobbing uncontrollably. I asked her all the obvious questions; what was the matter? where was her mother? was she in pain? and all the rest, but she just kept on sobbing. I spent a long time sitting on the bed trying to calm her down and eventually she began to get a bit more sensible. Between the sobs she eventually told me that her mum had just run out, which all seemed very odd. I decided that I would have to do something so got up and, looking out of the window, saw her mum coming slowly across the Square with Mrs B. At that time the Bs were the only people in the Square with a telephone and all emergencies were taken to them for a phone call. Talking to her later I got the other half of the story. The Queen had turned up on her doorstep gibbering away in hysterics. Eventually she calmed Queenie down enough to discover that 'S was haemorrhaging' and so she phoned for the doctor. Even then the Queen wouldn't go back home, she just wanted to wait until the doctor had called, but Mrs B managed to persuade her that she should go home and see how her daughter was. That was when I saw them. So I waited until they arrived and then left. The doctor eventually arrived and it turned out that she was just having a nosebleed but her mother had panicked.

The Queen was a diabetic and around the time we moved away she started to be very ill and have all sorts of complications. She was in and out of hospital and died very soon after. I have often wondered what happened to Mr H and S – they seemed such nice and inoffensive people to have to share a home with the Queen.

I can't remember who was in the flat under the Queen when we first moved in, but after a couple of years the Ws moved in. They also had one daughter, named after her mum. They were a nice couple and I still get a Christmas card from them every year. We had one close run in with them, though. One day I was coming in from work just as Mrs A (who lived in the bottom flat) was coming out of the door complaining about the smell of gas. She was right, the smell was awful! I made my way upstairs, trying to work out where the smell was coming from but it didn't seem so bad upstairs. I was only in for about ten minutes because I had some errands to run. I went straight out again, through the smell, downstairs, out and around the corner. For some reason I just glanced back at the flats, and noticed that the Ws' curtains were still drawn. Well, they weren't that sort of family at all so I went back and knocked up Mr K opposite. He was on afternoon shift that week and he knew the Ws a lot better than me. I must admit I was getting worried by now, and even more when he told me, in confidence, that Mrs W had left her husband a few days previously. So I looked through the letter box. The smell was awful, and sticking out of the kitchen was a pair of feet! Mr K grabbed the spare key he kept for them and we went in, turned off the gas cooker, opened all the windows, then called the ambulance. It was all touch and go, but he lived. Later they got back together again, and they still are.

The Ks were a nice family. They had lost their first baby and now had one boy, little T. He became a hairdresser and did quite well for himself. He bought a house out in Essex somewhere and later on his parents moved out to be near him. I don't know what became of them.

At the bottom were the As on one side and the Ms on the other. The As were older than everybody else in the flats, in fact the old man took his pension not long after we moved in. They had one grown-up son who used to visit quite often and keep an eye on them. Mr A died of a heart attack some time later, but then he always looked like a heart-case; short, fat, florid and always catching his breath.

The Ms weren't a happy family. They were Catholics and went to Mass every Sunday, but everything else about them seemed to be trouble. Mr M had the most awful temper and was always going on about somebody or something, shouting his mouth off, yelling at the kids in the Square and all the rest. Really he was a nasty piece of work. They had one daughter who they held up as the example of how children should be brought up, until suddenly she had to get married. The old man was beside himself, literally threw her out on the street and refused to speak or have anything to do with her or her husband. For years she used to visit her mum only when he was out of the house. Still, she seems to have made a decent marriage, and the last I heard she too was living out in Essex somewhere and her parents had moved out to be near her. I suppose there must have been some sort of reconciliation.

The Square was meant to be a sort of general community area and all the kids used to play there. It even had a basic kids' playground with a roundabout but they soon outgrew that and played on the grassed areas. At least it kept them off the streets, but there was always somebody ready to complain about the noise, or the danger of flying balls, or that they were ruining the grass or whatever. Looking back on it we had a taste of everything around that Square: friendships and feuds, romances, marriages and marriage break-ups, births and premature death, an attempted suicide, kids going into a life of crime and kids going to university and burglaries and great generosity. All in all, though, I wasn't one tiny little bit sad when we got the opportunity to move away into rural Essex. At least, that is how we thought of Basildon in the early 1960s.

Postscript

Mum's influence was long-lasting. Her grand-daughter Ruth read English at Fitzwilliam College, Cambridge University (1996–9). In 1998, as part of its celebration of fifty years of women receiving degrees, Cambridge University invited essays about the contribution of women to its development. This is an extract from 'Bounteous Mothers', Ruth's prize-winning essay.

* * *

Since the history books do not offer details of the lives of any of the women who served Cambridge in previous centuries, it is necessary instead to turn to a more recent example. Such an example is as valid as an older one, because even in this century, women have contributed to the successes of their sons, brothers and husbands more often than they have had the opportunity to earn those successes themselves. The woman in this example happens to be my grandmother, although many people in Cambridge today could probably tell their own equivalent stories.

My father came up to Cambridge in 1964. His parents were as nervous for him as they were proud; being working class people born and raised in the East End of London, Cambridge University must have seemed to them like a different world. Neither of them had stayed in school past fourteen. My grandmother had actually turned down a scholarship to the local girls' grammar school because her mother had insisted that 'no good ever came of book-learning'. Unfamiliar as the university system was to them, they supported my father in his application,

Fred and Polly at their Golden Wedding anniversary party in 1982.

and when they learned that he had been given a place, my grandmother used what knowledge she did have of Cambridge to give her son the best possible start at university. Having been evacuated to the village of Six Mile Bottom, near Cambridge, during the war, she had seen something of student life in the city. She had noticed that the students came up for term with their belongings packed into sturdy carriage-trunks, and so when my father took up his place at Cambridge in 1964, she used the money she had earned working as a cleaner to buy him a trunk just like those she had seen twenty years earlier.

Having gained his degree from Cambridge, my father was later able to send all three of his children to university. I am the last of them, and the trunk is still in use. It carries my belongings to and from college and then sits in my room all term serving as a coffee table. As the weeks go by, it gradually disappears under a growing mountain of unwashed mugs and unfiled lecture notes, but it is always there. It is, to me, a symbol of what one woman did, not only for her son, but for subsequent generations of her family and for the university itself, simply by supporting her son's wish to come to Cambridge.

The trunk is heavily battered now, and unlikely to survive beyond my graduation, but the legacy of my grandmother's support certainly will. Everything that I achieve in my life thanks to my education will also be thanks, in part, to her. So, too, will be any credit that the university gains from those achievements. She, and countless others like her, are the bounteous mothers of the alma mater.